THECLA MERLO
MESSENGER OF THE GOOD NEWS

Domenico Agasso

Thecla Merlo

Messenger of the Good News

St Paul MultiMedia Productions UK

Original title: *Tecla, antenna della "buona notizia"*
© 1993 Figlie di San Paolo, Rome

English translation by John Moore

St Paul MultiMedia Productions UK
Middle Green, Slough SL3 6BS

English edition © 1993 Daughters of St Paul, Great Britain

ISBN 0 9522538 0 1

Printed by The Guernsey Press Co Ltd, Guernsey, C.I.

The Daughters of St Paul are an international congregation of consecrated women serving the Church with the communications media.

Contents

Introduction

In 1994 the Daughters of St Paul celebrate the centenary of the birth of their first Superior General and Co-founder, Maria Teresa Merlo, or Maestra Thecla, as she was known in religion.

In 1915, when she was 21, the Holy Spirit opened before her a completely new future when he guided her steps towards Fr James Alberione in the town of Alba in Piedmont. In the previous year Fr Alberione had gathered around himself a group of young men with a view to promoting a mission which he had still not fully formulated – *the proclamation of the Gospel through the printed word and by all other means offered by the advance of modern technology.* He met Teresa on 27 June 1915 and told her of his intention of launching a congregation of women alongside the men, declaring his firm belief that they too were called to the mission of "the good press" as active partners in the pastoral work of the ordained priesthood. Teresa, who had already learned to see the hand of God in everyday events and to believe in the help of his "strong right arm", agreed to Fr Alberione's suggestion with enthusiasm. She knew she could count on God's help. So she and just two other young women came together as the first community of the future Daughters of St Paul. The group was born with scarcely a stir. Yet in that modest house in the Via Accademia at Alba they took the first steps towards the expression of their own charismatic character; they set up a tiny lending library with a prophetic name, "The New Book Shop". Not long afterwards they began to train as compositors, and in 1918 at Susa they finally moved into the field of their chosen calling by producing the diocesan newspaper, *La Valsusa.*

On 22 July 1922 Teresa was called by the Founder to lead the Congregation, which was constituted that day when the first nine sisters took vows, in which they promised to serve God and the Church for life through the apostolate of the printed word. For her name in religion she made the significant choice of Thecla, after one of St Paul's earliest followers.

From that day until 5 February 1964, when Our Lord accepted the offering of her life for the sanctification of the Daughters of St Paul, Thecla ceased to exist for herself. Her whole life became identified with that of the Congregation which she was called to guide in the ways of the spirit and of the modern apostolate.

We are indebted to Dr Dominic Agasso, who has combined the rigour of the historian with a journalist's fluency in his interpretation of original materials in the Pauline archives to give us a penetrating insight into the secret world of Maestra Thecla.

From this account there emerges the image of a simple and straightforward woman who treated the many extraordinary experiences of her life as entirely normal, never drawing attention to them, never losing her composure. Maestra Thecla remained her undemonstrative self–in the submissive manner of the Gospel servant–as she circled the globe several times by land, sea and air. The Daughters of St Paul set out under her guidance to explore all the complex means of social communication; and with the sole intention of doing good, of making Our Lord better known. It was a quest which soon led them to the use of previously untried methods, calling on them to combine their holiness as apostles with high professional skills.

Maestra Thecla's special charism was to know how to make herself available to others without interfering in their roles or losing sight of her own. Her particular greatness lay in the way she was able to work alongside the Founder, Fr James Alberione, whose boundless energy and enterprise more than kept pace with the speed of change in the twentieth century. She worked with him in the spirit of total faith, recognising a prophet of God. Such an idea as "the cult of personality" never entered her mind; indeed she remains a model and guide for today's apostles, giving a new impetus and providing a new dimension for the proclamation of the Gospel.

Thecla's message is still of great relevance today and the timely appearance of this fascinating account of her life will bring her many qualities to the attention of a wider public. We hope that her witness will offer encouragement to others, and that young people may be moved to consider the attractions of a vocation. She wished she had "a thousand lives to devote to the noble apostolate" of social communications. May she come to life again in these pages as witness and guide for a new generation of consecrated lives.

Sister Giovannamaria Carrara
Superior General
of the Daughters of St Paul

Foreword

Almost one hundred years after the birth of Maria Teresa Merlo and just over seventy years after she took vows as Maestra Thecla and became Superior General of the Pious Society of the Daughters of St Paul, Domenico Agasso has written the fascinating and definitive biography of this truly great woman.

The first subtitle of the first chapter probably best summarises the outstanding qualities of Mother Thecla, "A creative spirit rooted in obedience". She was obviously a woman of great personal strength of character, but one who sought to do not her own will but the will of God for the good of the Church. She was also a woman who was open to new initiatives and to truly creative projects in the service of the Gospel.

There is always a special providence evident in the lives of holy men and women; and the fact that the paths of Fr James Alberione and Maria Teresa Merlo crossed in the city of Alba is a providential moment in the history of the communications apostolate in the Catholic Church.

A foreword should not repeat the facts and insights of the book which it prefaces, but should perhaps offer a word of appreciation for the book itself and for its subject.

Mother Thecla was a truly great woman whose life story deserves to be widely known. This biography by Domenico Agasso not only traces the work of grace in her remarkable life but also provides a history of the origins and progress of the Daughters of St Paul, the religious congregation which has probably done more than any other group in the Church to make known the Gospel of Jesus Christ through the communications media.

May this book have the wide readership it deserves; and may the spirit of Maestra Thecla Merlo continue to inspire many young people to dedicate themselves to the exciting and creative work of proclaiming through the communications media the good news of Jesus Christ.

Most Rev John P Foley
President of the
Pontifical Council for Social Communication

Translator's note

Maria Teresa Merlo's name in religion, Thecla, is spelt in accordance with the Congregation's custom in English-language publications. Similarly Fr Giacomo Alberione is so well known as James to English speakers that he too has been made an exception to the rule that all Christian names, some of which have no clear English equivalent, are spelt as in their language of origin.

The title of *Maestra* by which Thecla was known throughout her life was originally intended by Fr Alberione to be used by all professed members of the Daughters of St Paul. The story is told in Chapter 2 under *The appointment of Maestra Thecla*. No single word in English conveys its precise blend of meaning, which extends across the notions of "teacher", "expert", "guide" and "model". The word also echoes the devotion to *Gesú Maestro*, Jesus the Master, a central element of Pauline spirituality.

As the international character of the Congregation increased over the years, more and more Daughters preferred to be known as Sister, and *Maestra* came to be used only of the older members of the Congregation. Few survived much beyond the second Vatican Council. Because of the frequency of direct quotations in which the word appears I have followed the author's convention of using it of those who were so called at the time they appear in the narrative. The title *Maestra* did not indicate any seniority, other than seniority of profession, over those who were known simply as Sister.

As the first Superior General, Thecla was also referred to as *Prima Maestra*.

Fr James Alberione was known both as the Founder and as *Primo Maestro*.

John Moore

Thecla Merlo
Messenger of the Good News

Chapter One

THE BEGINNINGS
OF A GREAT ADVENTURE

A creative spirit rooted in obedience

It was the spring of 1936. Among the passengers boarding the Italian liner *Augustus* at Genoa was the Mother General of a new institute of women, who was setting out to visit two of her houses in Brazil and Argentina. She would then sail north to the United States, where they had recently established another house. This nun's proposed itinerary would hardly have troubled the world's news desks. Yet if the names and circumstances of the people involved are filled in, the story begins to look strangely out of place in the twentieth century, for in reality theirs was an adventure typical of the Church in its earliest days.

The Mother General, known by the unusual title of *Maestra*, was Teresa Merlo. She had taken the name in religion of St Thecla, one of St Paul's first followers, and was now the head of the Daughters of St Paul, a new Congregation which was still waiting for pontifical approval, though it had already established three houses on the other side of the Atlantic. These had been founded by just two sisters in each country. All were Italians, and they had arrived without any knowledge of the language, with nowhere to live, and without any clear idea of how they might accomplish their mission. They had not been invited by the local hierarchy, who at first regarded them as a disturbing phenomenon rather than welcome helpers in the apostolate. Nuns who went about knocking on doors and offering books, pamphlets and leaflets for sale had not been seen before in those parts, and their missionary style was alien to local custom.

Their most dangerous leap in the dark had been the foundation of the house in New York. The two young nuns who stepped unsuspectingly off the boat in June 1932 were arriving at the worst possible moment. America was in the depths of the Great Depression, with tens of thousands of bankruptcies, 14 million unemployed, and everywhere queues at the soup kitchens. In the country districts farmers who had nothing left to hope for were abandoning their debt-ridden homesteads. In his native Illinois the future President Ronald Reagan left college to look for work because his father had lost his job, and the grocer would no longer give credit. Ruined businessmen sold apples on Fifth Avenue.

This was the situation that faced the two sisters as they embarked on their mission in the great metropolis. They knew no English, so they began by selling books to Italian immigrants. Their ultimate task would be to establish book centres and to organise a printing activity – though God alone knew how this was to be accomplished. They had left Italy with 4,000 Lire, quite a respectable sum for those times; but no sooner had they landed than they sent most of it back home, choosing to undertake their American mission and to face the economic blizzard with what they had earned from their apostolic work during the ocean crossing – just 90 Lire, or roughly a week's wages for an unskilled labourer.

On arriving in the New World, the sisters had received their first support from a small group of Italian priests of the Society of St Paul, of whom the Daughters were the sister organisation – two families of religious founded for the same purpose by the same man, a diminutive priest from Piedmont in north west Italy called James Alberione. It was he who had pioneered the method (if such it could be called) of simply throwing his young men and women upon the world, without invitation or guarantees of support, regardless of the suitability of the moment, and despite the misgivings of the many people who predicted failure, financial ruin and humiliation. Instead, the young Pauline Fathers and Brothers not only survived; they flourished, putting down firm roots and recording successes from the beginning.

Fr Alberione decreed at an early stage that there should be equality between the sexes, and he had no hesitation in placing women in the same front line positions as his men. He was confident that nuns of little more than twenty years of age could meet the challenge, and he refused to be swayed by accusations that it was foolhardy to send women into situations they had never faced before. He refused to be bound by the past, drawing on the Apostle Paul for his answer to all objections: "Forgetting the distance I have already covered, I reach forward and force myself towards the finishing line" (Phil 3:13-14).

In the course of a very few years his dream had become a reality; still a small reality, but already vibrant with life, and above all something that was recognised and valued. Those who at first had been shocked by the idea of two nuns crossing the world to sell books were soon calling for tens and indeed hundreds more of them to come to their countries and further God's work. What is more, in Latin America and the United States, this new interpretation of the female apostolate soon began to attract local vocations.

In this stage of his work Fr Alberione had the help of a very special woman, one who was able to enrich her religious obedience with singular creative gifts. This was Maestra Thecla, who now at the age of 42 was venturing beyond the shores of Italy for the first time. She meant to see all that the six pioneers had achieved on the other side of the Atlantic, work in which they had been encouraged by her frequent though usually brief letters, blending spiritual guidance with practical instructions about management of the shops, delivery details, pricing policy and book-keeping.

The notes on her journey are similarly brief, though they deal with a wide range of subjects, for Thecla was interested in everything new and was quick to adapt to unusual situations. Once on a coastal steamer she found that there was no chaplain, and so no Mass – even though it was

Corpus Christi. Her journal records her reaction, "I am the only religious on this boat, the only Italian, the only European. All the others are Americans; they speak English; one or two of them Spanish. So I have made a little altar in my cabin and in front of it I say my prayers, reading the Mass from my missal, meditating and making a spiritual Communion. On Sunday I even sang Vespers and I hope to do the same today."

All very calm and matter-of-fact; indeed so was her whole plan of life, which she expressed with her usual economy of phrase, "To make myself holy, but through commonplace things." In other words, to achieve the most difficult results by the most unremarkable means. Now that her work is over we can better understand the full significance of that expression. Thecla had the secret of transforming difficult and risky undertakings, with their burdens of weariness, worry and sorrow, into "commonplace things".

Her virtue was indeed "heroic", as is now confirmed by the solemn document signed on 22 January 1991 by John Paul II, marking the first step towards her canonisation as a Saint of the Church and recognising her achievement of the highest and most complete form of self-sacrifice.

So this is a story of true heroism – but heroism of an uncommon kind, acted out on a small scale and almost in silence, even in moments of the bitterest pain. She taught her Daughters, "I have learned that if we trust only in God and offer calm and untroubled obedience everything will turn out right, even when it may seem to us quite the opposite." Who knows how often it must have seemed quite the opposite to her during the dark hours as she was torn between the prospect of failure and the misery of being misunderstood? Above and beyond all this she had poor health to contend with all her life.

She also had to deal with many painful problems which were barely noticed at the time because she made so little fuss over them. These were the trials and tribulations that she tried to keep to herself, difficulties that she overcame and then made light of to the outside world as "common-place things", thanks to her enormous capacity for enlightened obedience. For she did not simply bow her head and comply woodenly; her obedience was rooted in the realisation that there are reasons that go beyond understanding, an obedience which fulfils itself by "leaving things to God". That is why her silent struggles went unnoticed by many of her colleagues, for throughout her trials Thecla was able to remain calm and untroubled. This was her real victory.

As already mentioned, the journey of 1936 was her first venture abroad, and apart from the interruption of the World War she was to travel the globe for the next 27 years. Meanwhile the sisters with their books and newspapers would multiply across the continents, always encouraged by her along the new paths indicated by the clear but exacting vision of Fr Alberione – a great father, master and prophet, but, like all prophets, an uncomfortable colleague and, for good measure, one endowed with inexhaustible energy.

With an organisation led and managed in this way there had to be someone to keep the group together, urging it on and at the same time smoothing the path of the women as they entered on an adventure which was new to them all, for they were the first in the history of the Church to take up the challenge of this kind of mission. There had to be someone like Thecla, someone who would never lose sight of the final destination, someone who would help them to refresh their spirits and lighten their burdens.

A quotation from 1930 gives some idea of what Fr Alberione intended his book centres to be and how he meant them to function. "They must be centres of the apostolate, points of contact backed by a supply of suitable material. We don't have a shop window so much as a banner fashioned from St Paul and the Gospel; not a point of sale, but a place where people are offered a service. We don't practise salesmanship, but the apostolate of the mind; we don't have customers, but rather disciples and collaborators; we aren't interested in business or financial returns, but in the gospel which spreads light and warmth around it. What matters is not what we take in payment, but what we offer as a gift. Our aim is not to control, but to offer humble collaboration with the Church. Our objective is not money, but souls."

That was his way. He wanted everything, and all of it straightaway – vertical take-off. These very demanding instructions were addressed to all the sisters, and Maestra Thecla passed them on without alteration. However, she showed the diplomatic touch by choosing as a heading "Guidance and encouragement", whilst at the end she added, "Read these words carefully, and bit by bit we shall get there. Don't get flustered; we will tackle this a little at an time. But meanwhile it is well to know what we are aiming to achieve." A perceptive and homely postscript that lent a encouraging familiarity to those rigorous marching orders.

Maestra Thecla was now just over 40 and in the prime of her life. But we have not yet given the customary description of her background, her childhood, her call to the religious life and the successive stages of the development of her vocation. The story is hard to tell in her case because her life followed no natural sequence.

She had wanted, even as a child, to join the Cottolengo Sisters, but was refused on account of her delicate health. This disappointment seemed to put an end to her hopes of becoming a nun and the years began to pass by. Quite unknown to her, however, unexpected developments were taking place in the Universal Church, even within a few miles of her own village, and it was because of them that this country girl was called on to tackle one of the most intractable problems of the Catholic world in the twentieth century.

The Church needed her for a venture so unprecedented that at first no one dared speak about it; indeed it still had no name. It would even involve her in working under cover: for long periods she was not free to speak about what she was doing. But her greatest surprise came when, one beautiful summer morning after a retreat, she and her companions took private religious vows; then, before nightfall, she found herself appointed head of her tiny community, the future Congregation of the Daughters of St Paul. She was thus in the situation of having to be her own novice mistress, to form and mature her own character as she went along, and to learn the arts of command by exercising them. Few women in the history of the Church have been faced with a comparable challenge.

She was blissfully unaware of the adventure in store as it began to take shape around her in the manner of an ancient rustic tale, with secret messages travelling at the speed of the letter-carrier and the ox-cart.

It all began when her name was first mentioned to Fr James Alberione, at that time a young priest, who was working on an idea which he dared not even mention because of the fears it might provoke.

A man of broad vision

This story really begins with Fr Alberione. The setting is the Province of Cuneo in lower Piedmont, an area of northern Italy bordering France, with plains fertile and well-watered and with hills made fruitful by the patience and ingenuity of generations of farmers, despite wars, invasions, revolutions and pestilence. The families of Michele Alberione and Rosa Teresa Allocco originated in the area of Bra, a town ten miles to the west of Alba, and locally celebrated as the home town of St Giuseppe Benedetto Cottolengo. They were tenant farmers, and had to move fairly frequently from one holding to another. It was whilst they were working in the plain of San Lorenzo di Fossano that James was born on 4 April 1884, the fourth of their five sons. Not long afterwards the family moved to Cherasco, also in the Province of Cuneo.

James was already talking about becoming a priest when

he was at school at Cherasco, and in fact he entered the junior seminary of the Archdiocese of Turin at Bra in October 1896. His first years passed unremarkably, though with excellent results. However in April 1900, at the age of 16, he experienced a serious crisis, which upset him so much that he left the seminary in the middle of the academic year. We do not know if he was unsettled by the endless and indiscriminate reading which he indulged in at that time, whether he was influenced by the example of some companion or if he found it hard to get along with his fellow-students. Nature had clearly not endowed him with the most docile of characters, for he was nick-named *fiammifero*, firebrand, referring to his easily aroused temper. The humility he later displayed was a hard-won conquest rather than a gift of nature.

However, in October of the same year he was back at his studies, this time at the seminary of Alba, the diocese in which the town of Cherasco lay. His re-admission had been made possible by the intervention of the parish priest, Fr Giovanni Battista Montersino, whose faith in this firebrand had never wavered. This time, after a period of observation, his studies ran their uneventful course through to his ordination in the Cathedral of Alba on 29 June 1907. Ten months later he was awarded his degree in theology at the Thomas Aquinas College at Genoa, and from that moment he became known to the whole diocese as *Il Teologo*, the Theologian, and was usually referred to by that sobriquet.

In the meantime he had begun to gain pastoral experience as assistant parish priest at Narzole; but in October 1908 the bishop who ordained him, Giuseppe Francesco Re, appointed him to the post of spiritual director of the seminary at Alba. It was then a city of some 14,000 inhabitants boasting a long history. A Roman settlement was founded there in the first century BC, and over the next thousand years, Alba gave to the ancient world and the Dark Ages both political adventurers and ambitious prelates, including a bishop who sided with the Emperor Henry IV against Pope Gregory the Great.

The office of spiritual director, to which Fr Alberione added teaching duties, is both sensitive and of fundamental importance to every seminary. Indeed it was about this time that Pope Pius X, with his keen interest in everything that concerned the formation of future priests, emphasised the importance of the role. So at the age of only 24, Fr Alberione, amid expressions of amazement and dismay, was placed in this position of great prominence. Many people questioned the bishop's wisdom in loading so much responsibility onto such immature shoulders.

However the bishop had made no mistake; indeed his choice was supported by an exceptional educator of priests, Fr Francesco Chiesa of Montà d'Alba, a graduate in dogmatic theology, in canon and civil law and in philosophy, who was well aware of all James Alberione's ideas and plans. He was to remain as spiritual director of the seminary until 1920, though he also undertook other duties: preaching in the churches of the diocese, often travelling on foot between villages, teaching catechism, advising on liturgy and taking part in Catholic social action over a wide area.

At the same time he was trying to develop another career, in parallel and in secret, one which he recalled as beginning during the historic night of 31 December 1900. The 90-year-old Pontiff Leo XIII had proclaimed a Jubilee Year, "now that the century is hastening to a close in which We, in God's mercy, have passed almost the whole of Our life". At midnight on that 31 December the whole Catholic world celebrated Mass, and afterwards the *Te Deum* was sung and the Blessed Sacrament exposed until dawn. The 16-year-old James Alberione, having by now overcome the crisis of his immaturity, spent those hours with his fellow seminarians in the Cathedral of Alba, whilst on its throne in the topmost niche of the lofty reredos the monstrance shone brightly as the world entered the twentieth century.

Later he was to recall those hours in which his new thoughts took shape. Speaking of himself in the third person, he said: "He felt a profound duty to prepare himself to do something for the Lord and for the men of the new age with whom he would have to live... He felt he had to work with others in the service of the Church... From then on these thoughts dominated his studies, his prayers, the whole of his priestly formation; and the idea, which at first had been rather confused, became clearer with the passing of the years and finally took shape in a specific project."

After a long period of careful reflection, Fr Alberione finally saw that what was needed was to make the Word of God accessible to the men and women of the new century, by using methods appropriate to the times and imparting a new vigour and efficiency to the task. At first he thought of setting up an informal partnership or guild with a voluntary apostolate of writers, printers and distributors to produce material inspired by Catholic teaching. Later he abandoned this idea in favour of something more radical: he would found a properly constituted religious congregation with its own rules and vows, but dedicated exclusively to this purpose, and with both male and female branches.

Women dedicated to a new apostolate

There was sure to be widespread nervousness, given the time and place, about involving women in the world of publishing; and though the project never left his mind Fr Alberione took care not to speak about it openly. Meanwhile he watched with interest the growing activity of the Catholic women's movement, the congresses, the publications, the cultural and social initiatives, and in 1911 he entered the debate himself with an essay entitled "The involvement of women in the holy mission of the priesthood", published as a book in 1915.

The title suggests that it was a *vade mecum* for the better use of women's contribution to parish life, and the book was certainly that, offering a wide selection of detailed examples. But the mission which the author wanted women to be involved in was of an apostolic kind, within the sanctuary and beyond, within and beyond the family. The female apostolate was needed everywhere. "It is not limited to charitable works, to improving the lot of working people. They must enlarge their field of operation to embrace the moral and religious healing of society." For example: "Nowadays a woman would not be doing her duty if she did not make sure that her children were receiving religious instruction at school."

The book also illustrates the sort of jobs that a woman might do both in Catholic publishing and in small scale distribution. But it then goes on to assert that there is no aspect or function of the apostolate of the printed word from which the efforts of women should be excluded. "To begin with, a woman of suitable background can at least write."

Fr Alberione made no reference in his book to his own project, avoiding premature challenges to the short-sighted vision of so many of his contemporaries. But he did take up a strong position alongside those who were trying to free Catholic life and action from the prevalent spirit of passive acquiescence. "Let us not be counted among those who have resigned themselves... We are not afraid... Ours is the twentieth century, and it is in this century that we must live and work. We have to be people of the age, trying to understand its needs and to exert ourselves to meet them. In these days it takes organisation to produce results. Well then, let us organise righteousness; let us marshall men of goodwill. People are trying to encourage a love of reading, so let us make sure that there is a supply of wholesome material to read. Nowadays it seems that almost anyone can get up and speak on any subject; let us prepare ourselves so that we also can speak out... And since we are people of our own time let us make sure that women too are prepared for the new age."

Only one man knew the difficulties, the growing pains, the halting progress of Fr Alberione's plans, his friend and

23

spiritual advisor, Francesco Chiesa, parish priest of SS Cosmas and Damian, a canon of the Cathedral of Alba, and one of the most influential men in the diocese. They met to talk over ideas, plans, strategies and tactics, careful in choosing the right moment for every new move, just as farmers in the nearby hills took note of changes in the weather before deciding on the day's work.

A most significant development occurred in September 1913, when Bishop Re decided to launch Fr Alberione into the world of publishing. He appointed him editor of the *Gazzetta d'Alba*, the diocesan weekly founded in 1882 by the far-sighted Bishop Lorenzo Pampirio. It was one of the first publications of its kind in Italy. The circulation was 1,500 copies when he took over, but Alberione was to raise this to 9,000 in the course of a few years. This was his first personal contact with the press. It was also a brief foretaste of his life's work, which began in earnest the following year.

The summer of 1914 saw one of the most disastrous failures of international order in recent times. On 28 June the hereditary Archduke of the Austro-Hungarian Empire and his wife were assassinated at Sarajevo, and the Serbian government was accused of complicity in the crime. Serbia rejected the Austrian ultimatum, and on 28 July the Empire declared war.

Just four days before, on 24 June, Fr Alberione had purchased two printing presses from the Turin firm of Nebiolo, paying for them in gold coin and installing them at Alba in a house in Piazza Cherasca (today's Piazza Mgr Grassi).

It seemed that all Europe was going mad. On 1 August Germany declared war on Russia, and two days later on France. Britain declared war against Germany on the fifth, and the Austrians against Russia on the following day. Finally, on 11th and 13th of the month, France and Great Britain declared war on Austria.

Against this background of chaos Fr Alberione chose 20 August, the day on which Pope Pius X died, to found the

Society of St Paul, an organisation destined to spread its presence and influence over the whole world. At that moment however it consisted of just two young men learning their trade from a master compositor. It also had an ambiguous and safe-sounding name, the Young Workers' Printing School. It looked no more than an obscure little business in a house which served as both lodging and workplace.

He had six young men by the end of 1914, and after several changes of address the operation settled more permanently, with presses in one place and living quarters in another. By the spring of 1915 the original premises in Piazza Cherasca had been vacated, and Fr Alberione decided that this would be an ideal place to establish his girls and young women.

But what girls and young women? And what were they to train for? For the time being Fr Alberione offered inquisitive visitors no more than a rather evasive name. The sign on the premises of the former Printing School read simply "Women's Workshop". It opened on 15 June 1915, three weeks after Italy entered the war against Austria.

This was the true date of birth of the Daughters of St Paul, though for the moment they had no formal existence – not even a name. In the workshop at that time there was only Angela Maria Boffi, a woman of 29 who had been employed as a secretary by a local wine shipper. She had originally wanted to join an enclosed order, and she undoubtedly possessed the necessary determination and austerity of mind; but she had shown her generosity of spirit by giving up that dream to care for her sick mother. She was a catechist in the parish of Canon Chiesa, and he it was who had drawn her to the attention of Fr Alberione as the right kind of person for his project.

The next task was to find more female recruits. And here the problem was different from that of finding young men. The first of these to follow him, logically enough, were boys he had known and helped to guide as church students. But it was another matter entirely for the spiritual director of a seminary to set up a women's workshop, install a secretary from a winery and set about looking for other young women to join her. A growing number of the diocesan clergy were worried that Alberione was beginning to cause scandal, for they understood neither his project nor the reaction of the bishop, who simply watched and held his peace. Alberione was not yet free to reveal that he was setting in motion what was intended to become an engine for the production of priests, religious brothers and sisters of a new kind, devoted to the press, publishing and whatever else might be needed for evangelisation in the decades to come.

The bishop refused to take sides, simply hoping that these ideas were "of God" (Acts 5:34-39). Canon Chiesa meanwhile encouraged his superior to take a favourable view and supported the project. Alberione himself spent many hours on his knees, from which he often arose with yet another page of his programme firmly implanted in his mind.

His female recruits certainly represented a completely new page, for there was no seminary to draw on; they had to be found in their own homes. This was not the path followed by other girls, who entered the convents of established congregations by following well-defined procedures. Here it was a case of inviting girls and young women to sew military uniforms, for which Fr Alberione had secured a contract. Later there was the possibility of becoming a different kind of nun in a different kind of world, guided by rules which had still to be written, performing a task that no one had yet undertaken.

Vocations were still plentiful at that time; many families had aunts who were nuns, and they were able to guide young aspirants with advice and by example. But these nuns did not have that kind of aunt; they were originals, owing nothing to any tradition. In addition they had to pass the test of an extremely laborious period of trial complicated by the need to operate partly under cover.

So it was necessary to search out the first recruits one by one and to look not only for all the usual qualities required for the religious life but also for that special kind of courage needed to face a new kind of work. The first young women to accept the challenge would have a fundamental influence on the future community, for they would set the example with which those who came later would identify.

As he pondered over this problem, Fr Alberione paused on the name of a young woman who had been mentioned to him; it seemed somehow familiar – Teresa Merlo. Her village, Castagnito, was quite close, only a couple of hours' journey from Alba.

Teresa, sewing teacher and catechist

The Merlo family of Castagnito consisted of father and mother, Ettore and Vincenza (née Rolando), and their four children: Giovanni Battista, born in 1892, Maria Teresa, born on 20 February 1894, Costanzo Leone and Carlo, who arrived in 1896 and 1898. The war was to involve the three sons in turn, including Costanzo Leone, who was then at the seminary and who later served many years as parish priest of Barolo, home of Piedmont's most famous wine. Giovanni Battista and Carlo grew up to work the family farm under the watchful eye of their father.

The Merlo family farmed on their own account and were among the more technically aware of their generation: farming magazines were read in the house and they kept bees. Even Teresa's sewing machine was the most up-to-date model – indeed perhaps the only one for miles around.

In other words it was a family which stood out from its background, but not because of any particular wealth or position. Rather, the esteem and authority they enjoyed were based on the only things that counted in the countryside of those days: fields that were among the most carefully tended, a law-abiding and happy family, moderation in speech. They were a family with generations of proud self-sufficiency behind them. It was natural that many of the village folk should seek Ettore's advice on farming, family and business matters. He was in effect the unadorned, rustic personification of the Just Man, a man of work and of faith, the same Christian when he joined in the hymns at Vespers as when he stood in his fields or in the market-place at Alba. It was also typical of Italian country ways that the virtues of his wife Vincenza – she was about her business from dawn to dusk – were counted to his credit. The children were regular attenders at all church functions, particularly at the catechism classes of Fr Pistone, the parish priest; but first and foremost it was in their own home, from Ettore and Vincenza, that they learned the principles of the Christian life.

This was the domestic background into which Maria Teresa (or simply Teresa as she was known in the family) was born and in which she grew up. At Castagnito she completed the first three classes of the primary school – the only ones the village provided – and in the final examinations her marks were well above average: 9 in written Italian, 9 in reading, 10 in arithmetic, 9 in history, geography and the rights and duties of the citizen, 7 in handwriting.

To continue her schooling Teresa had to go to Guarene, nearly two miles away, but after the first few months she decided to stay at home and interrupt the fourth year of her studies. The risk of catching an infection in winter was too high for a young person of her frail constitution, which called for special diet and daily doses of a special tonic preparation. Her mother had nevertheless insisted that she should continue her studies with a private teacher at Castagnito, Maria Chiarla. Under her guidance Teresa completed the syllabuses of the fourth and fifth years ahead of schedule. But that was not all. As Luigi Rolfo has recorded in his memoir *Alle sorgenti*, Maria Chiarla did much more for her pupil. "With the full approval of Teresa's parents she helped her towards a better understanding of the spiritual life, and in particular she taught her to make a short meditation each day, providing her with a book which Teresa held particularly dear and which she still kept after she entered the religious life".

Clearly, this child had more important gifts than the intelligence indicated by her school results. She stood out among girls of her own age and had no difficulty in establishing confident relationships with adults. After her period under Maria Chiarla she came under the wing of a Miss Cassinelli, a wealthy woman of the neighbourhood, and thanks to her, Teresa was able to make occasional visits to the mountains, with consequent benefit to her health. They also went together to stay with the nuns of Maria Auxiliatrix at Nizza Monferrato, where they undertook various spiritual exercises.

She made her First Communion at eight, was confirmed at thirteen, and attended Mass and received Communion daily. She led the singing in church and was practising as a catechist well before the normal age. In short, there were all the characteristic signs of a future nun. And indeed in her home village there were the Cottolengo Sisters, who ran the nursery school, and offered the natural focus for her ambitions. However, for the health reasons already alluded to, Teresa could never have contemplated donning their habit.

So to assure her independence in all future eventualities she had to learn a trade. She was not content to achieve a sufficiency in just any kind of job; she had to be one of the best, like her father and brothers on the farm. In those days, given her poor health, there was not much for a girl to choose from. Sewing and embroidery were the most obvious choices, and to learn these she had to leave home for a time. Her first school was the Retreat House of the Divine Providence Nuns in Alba, where sewing of a very high standard was taught. She then moved to Turin to study to become an embroidery teacher. Altogether she spent two years away from home, which involved considerable sacrifices for her family, but she returned to Castagnito happy in the knowledge that she had mastered a skill that would virtually guarantee her future.

Her training enabled her to open a workshop and school of sewing and embroidery in the family home, and she was soon teaching groups of pupils, many of them from the surrounding villages. Some were complete beginners; others wanted to improve their skills, and some came just to prepare their trousseaux. Today we might almost say that she was running a studio. For Teresa however there was also a further dimension; her pupils were to become both good seamstresses and good Christians. For her a job well done, a prayer well said, an explanation fully understood, a poor person helped, an unfriendly gesture forgiven were all parts of the same whole. She was unable to imagine one without the others; like her father Ettore, the same exemplary Christian when he was pruning his vines as when he took his regular place in the choir at Vespers.

The pupils for their part, as often happens with an admired teacher, began unconsciously to imitate her good manners, and the choice of sewing mistress was quite frequently dictated by this consideration. To be able to say, "I was taught by Miss So-and-so" also meant having learned her standards of behaviour. And those who learned from Teresa revealed the fact in small acts of kindness and general refinement of manner which could be traced directly to her.

As for Teresa herself, she was unconsciously preparing herself for something much more ambitious, though for the moment she was probably content in her teaching and with the happiness that her work as a catechist brought her. Well before her twentieth birthday she had already been noted by her parish priest as the best prepared and most effective of his teachers.

Castagnito and Fr Pistone, like the whole diocese of Alba, its bishop and many of its priests, were in the vanguard in the matter of religious instruction at a time of widespread and profound religious ignorance. The Catholic world was riven by controversy, with bitter attacks from the Modernists being countered by robust defensive tactics. Individual bishops and synods complained of a falling away from true doctrine and from the systematic teaching of the Faith, but this was certainly not the fault of the faithful when religious instruction was neglected even in certain junior seminaries.

Moreover there was the tragic influence of current social conditions. As their bishops and parish priests wrote: "The long working hours imposed on the young, which often exceed their powers of endurance, make it impossible for them to take part in catechism classes. The Po delta affords a particular example: young people there cannot attend these classes in winter because they lack proper clothing and footwear, whilst in summer they are busy working in the fields." (L Nordera, *The Catechism of Pius X*, Ed LAS)

In April 1905 Pope Pius X himself took up the sad theme in his encyclical *Acerbo nimis,* in which he wrote: "It is a common and justified complaint in these times that among today's Christians there are many who live in an extreme state of ignorance of those matters which are essential for their eternal salvation... We know that the office of catechist is poorly understood in many quarters; it is commonly held in low esteem and is not accorded the credit it deserves... As a result, the Faith has grown faint in our days, to the point where it has almost completely faded, and the duty of teaching the catechism is fulfilled, if at all, with great superficiality." His Holiness ordered, "that every parish priest, and all those who in any way have responsibility for the cure of souls, should, on every Sunday and holiday of obligation of the year without exception, spend one hour instructing the young children in their care on the text of the catechism".

The Alba diocese had no need to be prompted, having led the way in this matter for decades. Alba had been well represented at the national congress on catechetics at Piacenza in 1889, and had immediately put into practice the chief recommendation by establishing a school for religious teachers. In those days the catechism most widely used was the one originally compiled in 1765 by Bishop Casati of Mondovì, and in a revised edition of 1896 it became the approved text for religious instruction in all the dioceses of Piedmont and Lombardy. After 1912, when the universal catechism of Pius X was published, Alba was prompt in bringing its practices up to date, instituting a diocesan catechetical commission for the training of teachers in the new programmes and methods.

It undoubtedly says something for the state of awareness in this tiny diocese that clergy meetings called to discuss the catechism were attended by as many as 150 priests. But perhaps a small incident from military life illustrates the results of this to greater effect. Two Alba seminarians who had been called to the colours were taking part in a barrack room discussion about religion and they listened in amazement to a well-argued defence of Catholicism by a private soldier. They afterwards approached him in the belief that he must be at least a church student or perhaps even a priest, only to discover that he was a country boy with nothing more behind him than a primary school education. He had received his catechetical instruction in the diocese of Alba, in fact at Castagnito at the hands of Fr Pistone. His name was Giovanni Battista Merlo, and it was through him that the two students became acquainted with the whole family. It was natural that they should speak about them to Fr Alberione, who thus came to hear about Teresa, the sewing mistress and catechist, at that time 22 years of age. One of the Merlo sons, Costanzo Leone, was a student at the seminary, and it was through him that Fr Alberione made his approach to the mother. Would she perhaps permit Teresa to teach sewing and catechism at Alba in the newly opened workshop?

Vincenza Merlo can hardly have been impressed by this suggestion, for her daughter was already doing precisely that in her own home. However they had a family discussion and finally decided to have Fr Alberione explain to them in person what he had in mind. So on Sunday, 27 June 1915, there was a meeting at Alba in the church of SS Cosmas and Damian. Fr Alberione took aside first the mother and then the daughter into the sacristy – separate conversations with a single purpose. He explained that he was looking for someone to guide the small band which was sewing clothing for the army. But that was by no means all; his hope was that something completely different would emerge from the group and their experiment of a life in common. For Teresa this was an utterly unexpected chance to realise her dream of becoming a nun. It was to be something quite new; it would take time, and she would need to wait patiently and to pray.

Teresa accepted, having previously obtained her mother's approval, as was the custom in the Merlo household. She remained behind in Alba that Sunday so that she could start immediately. Having nowhere to live in town, she stayed with the Boffi family for a few months; and then at the end of 1916 more suitable premises were found in Via Accademia, which became both lodgings and workshop.

Angela Maria Boffi had another job and could devote only a few hours a day to the project, whilst Teresa Merlo was able to work there full time, though on the same level as the others, doing exactly the same work. As time passed she began to emerge as leader on account of her competence as a seamstress and because of certain spiritual qualities of which her companions gradually became aware. Slowly but surely the life of the small group was steered in the direction intended by Alberione. From the very beginning its members were guided towards the community life, their future vows and the new apostolate of the printed word. Guided by the spiritual counsels of Fr Alberione and Canon Chiesa, the group began, in prayer and meditation, to take on its own special character. The girls whose interest lay only in craft training were lost by the way, but others took their places, attracted by the prospects of the religious life.

The outward appearances of the operation were still disguised to avoid unwelcome curiosity. The advertisements in the *Gazzetta d'Alba* spoke of the school in Via Accademia as teaching sewing, tailoring and embroidery – Fr Alberione was always careful to avoid any description that might arouse curiosity – and the same announcements also made it known that good books could be found at the same address.

The numbers involved should not be exaggerated. After an unfortunate start with the military contract, which seems to have gone wrong because of a mistake on the part of the army authorities, the school settled down to offering craft training to external students, whilst only those in residence followed the "Alberione course" towards the religious life and the apostolate of the printed word. The numbers were indeed small; there were just three on 16 February 1916, four at the beginning of April 1917 and only five a year later. These figures come from the reports which Fr Alberione sent periodically to the bishop, reports in which he always speaks of "daughters" in the Piedmontese sense of young girls. Few enough, in all conscience! It seemed that the project was having difficulty in getting under way. It was also heading towards stormy waters for other reasons.

And what a storm there was! Today it is almost impossible to imagine that such things could happen. First the bishop was asked to bring the experiment to an end. Then when this achieved nothing people wrote to the Vatican Congregations calling for the suppression of the project. And as if this were not enough, others tried to involve the civil authorities, including an Under-Secretary in Rome, so intent were they on destroying the small, almost invisible, achievements of two small groups of young men and women.

The reason for this fierce opposition was one which is unfortunately not unknown today. Fr Alberione's opponents were well-intentioned Christians, not enemies of the Church bent on uprooting it. In their eyes it was he who was the wrecker, "Public Enemy Number One". They accused him of undermining the seminary by enticing its students into a risky project, which also involved girls and young women who had been taken from their families or diverted from religious orders where they would have been better employed. And it must be acknowledged that many of his recruits came from parishes where they were already doing excellent work – young women like Teresa Merlo, the most effective catechist of Fr Pistone, who was never to forgive James Alberione for taking her away.

Then again, considering the unhappy results of other Catholic ventures into the world of journalism and publishing, did not this whole costly business, with its printing machinery, its raw materials, its costly premises, represent a dreadful financial risk? Those who asked these questions were not motivated by malice. They were good people who were unable to take the long view. For them Fr Alberione was a dangerous man who for the good of the diocese had to be stopped at any cost. It is perhaps to be marvelled at that the two small groups of seminarians and "daughters" managed to persevere in the face of such opposition. Teresa herself was later to write: "At times we were so discouraged that we hardly knew which way to turn."

It was inevitable that gossip should get back to their families. Clelia, the third young woman to join, wrote home to her mother: "I'm not afraid of what they say because I know what I'm doing and what this place is all about. As the proverb says: 'Speak no evil, do no evil, and let the sparrows twitter.' I thank God that I've experienced more peace and tranquillity here than you could ever imagine, and I really don't care what people try to say about us."

Training for the responsibilities of pioneers

All the young women persevered, thanks to Fr Alberione's way of handling the problem. The attacks, however much they provoked his fiery temperament, never upset the good relations he maintained with his young people. Despite all difficulties, reversals of fortune and accidents – they even had an outbreak of fire in the house – he never played the part of the victim, preferring to talk about lack of faith, and in particular of his own. "There are only two things that really bother me", he told his group during a meditation in 1918, "and that is that I'm not yet good enough, and you aren't yet holy enough. These are my only two anxieties. I don't have any others. In the end nothing else matters."

Such a direct approach was not calculated to make his young men and women feel comfortable, but it did give them an awareness of their responsibilities as people who would be called on to break new ground. It was the starting point in the formation of apostles who must be ready to set off in any direction without help or support and to face obstruction even from fellow Catholics. This was his way of bracing them to resist the temptation of self-pity, of encouraging them to "think big", even whilst they were still operating on a scale so small as to be almost invisible, when the future apostles of the printed word could be counted on the fingers of one hand.

Fr Alberione's reports to the bishop give some idea of the way the group functioned. As early as February 1916 they had begun a small bookstall, run by the girl who looked after the crèche attached to the workshop. They were trying to be as self-sufficient as possible, and so they had to fend for themselves in the preparation of their food. They also found that they must provide a qualified primary school teacher, and this task was entrusted to Angela Boffi, supported by Fr Alberione, who was able to announce to the bishop in 1918 that she had passed her examinations and was about to start training three of her colleagues.

Meanwhile the list of jobs they were prepared to undertake became ever longer, as one of their advertisements proclaims: "Workshop for non-resident women, sale of religious books and devotional supplies, instruction in catechism, typesetting". So now the young women were coming to grips with the craft of printing. The Young Workers' Printing School was already established; its young apprentice compositors and printers were to become priests, the new men of the apostolate. Now the same path beckoned to the "daughters". Indeed their initiation was almost immediate; from the beginning they were undertaking jobs such as the folding and hand stitching of books and the packing and despatch of parcels. Finally in 1917 they graduated to typesetting, starting with a single apprentice and just three staff. Fr Alberione had the title of Manager, Miss Boffi was Manageress, and Teresa Merlo the assistant – with a small "a".

The girls and young women in residence were members of the parish of SS Cosmas and Damian and not merely in the performance of their spiritual duties. Canon Chiesa, parish priest since 1913, launched a revolutionary scheme for the teaching of religion. It was a three-year course based on weekly conferences for the training of future teachers of catechists, with annual examinations leading to a final certificate of competence. This was followed by a fourth year of twice-monthly conferences dealing with the spiritual life.

In August 1914 he also founded in the parish a League of Catechists, and it is clear from its constitution that the training of its members was intended to have a strong spiritual dimension, involving retreats, daily meditation, visits to the Blessed Sacrament and activities which today would be described as voluntary work.

This was the background against which the first "daughters" made their early progress in the spiritual life, in particular Angela Boffi, the oldest among them, and Teresa Merlo, who followed the first of these courses from its second year to the fourth. In addition there was the personal counsel of Fr Alberione, who went regularly to the workshop to give instruction and to hold discussions. He conducted these very simply without desks or benches, sometimes in the work area itself, sometimes in the kitchen.

He once gave a talk on the philosophy of Thomas Aquinas to the young men of the Printing School whilst helping to prepare a meal of maize porridge.

Speaking of the men, there is a date of historic importance to record. After they had qualified as printers, these seminarians took their first step towards the religious life. In the Printing School on 8 December 1917, the feast of the Immaculate Conception, four of them stood before Fr Alberione, vested in his surplice and stole, to renew together the private vows which they had taken separately at different times before. This important step was marked in the traditional manner by their adopting the names of their chosen patron saints: Giuseppe Giaccardo (Timoteo), Michele Ambrosio (Domenico), Desiderio Costa (Giovanni Crisostomo), Bartolomeo Marcellino (Paulo) and Torquato Armani (Tito).

On 29 June 1918, the feast of SS Peter and Paul, the young women took a similar step, when they also came together to renew the private vows they had previously made as individuals. There were just three of them – Angela Maria Boffi, Teresa Merlo and Clelia Caliano – in a brief and almost conspiratorial early morning ceremony. Their companions knew nothing about it until later: Fr Alberione was the only person present besides themselves. It would be a long time yet before they would be seen as religious in the eyes of others.

Yet Teresa had no anxieties, not even those that sometimes beset the saints themselves. She knew well enough that spiritual progress could not be speeded up to order; nor was she one to suffer from home-sickness or pine for the relatives left behind. She had made a carefully pondered choice, and for that reason there was never any question of regret. Rather, she drew strength from the affectionate memory of her family and from the love with which they had surrounded her, particularly during her sickly childhood. Now in her letters to her parents there was a special eagerness to draw upon the peace and calm of her new state in order to repay something of what she had received from them.

Here is something she wrote to her mother in the summer of 1916: "My dearest Mother, I would like to say so many beautiful things to you on the feast of your patron saint, but I just can't express what I feel. Certainly it wasn't without a painful farewell that you let your Teresa go (let her go, not sent her away)... Since I already say a prayer for you each day – no, several times a day – you can imagine the special warmth of my prayers on your feast day... I want my mother to have all the graces she wishes for herself, for her sons in the army and for those other sons who are nearer to her."

The subject of her brothers at the war prompts her to write to her father: "Dear Father, you too need consolation and encouragement, don't you? Once again I feel the need to thank you for the Christian upbringing you gave me; I value it very much, and I'm more and more grateful to you for it every day."

In 1918, the last year of the war, a terrible influenza epidemic, the so-called Spanish flu, exploded and spread over practically the whole of Europe, even reaching the United States. There were hundreds of thousands of deaths among the millions affected. Once soldiers' families lived in dread of the fatal telegram from the front telling them that a son had been killed in battle; now it was the soldiers who went in fear of tragic news from home. The Spanish flu struck without mercy, carrying away young and old, the infirm and the able-bodied, without distinction.

In the workshop Clelia Calliano, as well as being the most cheerful member of the group, was without doubt the young woman with the strongest constitution. Hailing from Corneliano d'Alba, she had been among the first to join, and entered with equal enthusiasm into all the activities, whether she was trying to master the finer points of printing or cleaning up in the kitchen. She was just 26 when the epidemic took her from them. She died on the evening of 22 October 1918 with her companions standing round her bed reciting the fifth glorious mystery of the Rosary. According to the seminarian Giuseppe Giaccardo, Clelia had murmured these words to Fr Alberione before dying: "If the Lord spares me I want to devote all my energy to 'the good press'. Even if I only look after the cooking and sweep out the place where the other girls work I think that would still be a great vocation. And if I have to die I offer my life for the cause of this apostolate".

To Susa as though to Bethlehem

Clelia died whilst Fr Alberione was already thinking about a new departure, but her death did not halt his plans; indeed it seemed more urgent, something that could be dedicated to her memory. He had received a proposal from Bishop Giuseppe Castelli of the Alpine diocese of Susa, on the border between the province of Turin and France. The bishop wished to resume the publication of *La Valsusa*, a diocesan weekly which had been suspended for lack of staff, and he proposed that Alberione should send his young women to Susa to restart the operation. (He probably had no idea that only one of those at Alba was capable of setting type and that none of them knew much about layout.) But when Fr Alberione put the situation to them in its most discouraging light Teresa Merlo did not hesitate; she replied with complete confidence, "Tell the bishop you accept." And this was the view of them all.

Fr Alberione's parting message does not seem by our standards to have been calculated to encourage: "Off you go! You will stay in Susa for three or four years; you will work in silence; and then the good Lord will make something of you". All the same, Susa rarely welcomed a happier group of young women than this – five of them in all, rich in their poverty and looking forward to their first winter among the mountains.

Chapter Two

THE NEW NAME

The move to Susa was an abrupt transplant of the seedling organisation. Whilst Fr Alberione was mounting an offensive on all fronts on behalf of the men of the Society of St Paul, the tiny group of young women left Alba to develop in a more sheltered atmosphere. Though they had been invited to Susa to perform a specific task and enjoyed official patronage, they were still to encounter rough treatment, though nothing on the scale of their experiences at Alba.

On 16 December 1918 an advance party, consisting of Angela Boffi and Bartolomeo Marcellino, set out for Susa. At that time Marcellino was little more than a raw seminarian-printer, though Fr Alberione was later to send him to the other side of the world, to Japan, where he would win fame with his network of radio stations. The others followed two days later: Teresa Merlo, the compositor Emilia Bianco, Caterina Petean (a refugee from the war-zone in Friuli) and Mariuccia Prinotti. The last three were not much more than thirteen years of age. Two other girls arrived later, Enrichetta Morando and Maria Delpiano. Even at its maximum strength the community at Susa would number only twelve.

"In Antioch", we read in the Acts, "the disciples were for the first time called Christians" (Acts 11:26), and for the young girls the city of Susa assumed something of the same significance, for something similar happened there. Although they wore no distinctive dress, people quickly came to recognise them as they moved between their house, the printing press, the church, and a book shop they had re-opened. In this shop they set up a large painting of the Apostle Paul, and it was because of this picture that they came to be known – first in the local patois and later in

Italian – as the Daughters of St Paul. And the name, with its wealth of literal and spiritual overtones, was to remain with them thereafter. The Daughters were to be followers and imitators of the Apostle whose life's work had been to proclaim Christ.

Before long the whole city, starting with the bishop himself, had taken this brave little band to their hearts. Yet they lived in very dilapidated quarters and did nothing to make themselves more comfortable. Their living conditions quite dismayed the new bishop, Mgr Umberto Rossi, when he first visited them with one of his priests in 1921. Later he wrote: "I have never seen such a poor and wretchedly furnished lodging as that first little house where Sister Thecla Merlo lived with her fellow aspirants to the religious state." There was not even enough room for the regular practice of prayer and meditation; they made the best of a bad job by using each of the local churches in turn.

As long as they won the battle to bring out *La Valsusa* they were happy to accept any privations and to postpone all improvements in their conditions. This tiny group of young girls, who until now had no experience of layout, page-design or newspaper production, was absolutely determined that the diocesan weekly should be re-launched, and as soon as possible. They gave notice to all – reporters, feature writers and correspondents – that they must have their material ready in time for a first issue in early January.

It is easy to imagine their frustration as they struggled for the first time with contributors' scripts, reams of paper and above all machinery, which seemed undecided whether to help or to hinder their efforts. There were days and nights of painstaking labour, experiments, failures, checks and double-checks, and many anxious prayers. Lawyers and other professionals who arrived with their articles were astonished to find, not a team of experienced compositors headed by some imperiously knowledgeable foreman, but a handful of girls. When the electricity failed, Teresa had to turn the presses with her own hands – hands which until then had been occupied chiefly with sewing and embroidery. Perhaps those priests and other dignitaries of Alba were right after all when they said James Alberione was out of his mind.

Somehow the battle was won: *La Valsusa* came out punctually in the first days of January 1919. The circulation of that issue was barely 500 copies, but it mattered little. What counted was that the diocese had a voice of its own again, an event of cultural as well as religious importance and a source of pride to everyone.

The Daughters quickly consolidated their place in the affections of the townsfolk. Indeed the extent of this was demonstrated when, on a November night in 1919, fire swept through their lodgings, destroying most of the furniture. Teresa recalled it in these words: "As soon as it became known in town that we had had a fire, many well-disposed families came forward to help. Some offered to lend us anything we might need; others wanted to take us into their homes. We were all very moved by the way they supported us." And the citizens of Susa showed their consideration in other ways. "We were sometimes careless in leaving the door of the shop open during the lunch break, yet we never lost so much as a sheet of paper. On one occasion the neighbours roused us in the middle of the night to tell us we had forgotten to lock up."

Teresa was simply not strong enough to work the machinery by hand during the repeated emergencies and so a young boy was brought over from Alba. In any case her energies were needed for more important things, because by then she was beginning to take charge of every aspect of the work.

One of the contributors to *La Valsusa* was a Turin lawyer by the name of Luigi Chiesa, a journalist with many productive years behind him, whose professional judgements were the more respected for being invariably expressed with great candour. His weekly visits to Susa gave him ample opportunity to observe Teresa Merlo at work, and he has left this description of her at that time: "I have never forgotten her painstaking attention to detail and imaginative suggestions during those years when we were trying to improve the paper. Nothing was too much trouble for her to ensure that the production process went smoothly. She took the most scrupulous care in correcting proofs, in the selection of appropriate typefaces for headlines (though in truth there were not many to choose from) and in the supervision of the print run. Those young girls performed miracles under her leadership, particularly considering their lack of experience and the very limited equipment at their disposal. All this was crucial to the continuous growth in circulation that we achieved."

Fr Alberione had told them that they were to work a few years at Susa in silence; however he did not leave them quite alone. There were regular exchanges of correspondence, and every summer he and Canon Chiesa came over to spend a few days with them so that each girl could speak in confidence and talk through any problems or difficulties she might have.

These meetings were also occasions for a kind of lawmaking. The group was a congregation in embryo and so it had no tried and tested Rule of its own. There were few analogies with other female communities because the purpose for which this group had come together was quite new; everything was being done for the first time, without the help of precedents or established procedures.

This made it especially necessary for Fr Alberione to come to Susa in person; for the moment he himself was the Rule. He never embarked on these community discussions with his young ladies without first spending an hour or so in prayer. His decisions and suggestions in matters of order and discipline all derived from one basic idea – which was already the essence of a Rule – namely, that women no less than men had a vocation to the mission and like men they had to go into action in the front line. They were not merely to act as housekeepers. And so in this informal way all their problems were slowly resolved, with each new idea being evaluated in the light of the underlying principle and adopted or abandoned accordingly.

The young women recognised God's will for them in the words of James Alberione. They knew that the only possible response was that of Abraham in the Old Testament and of St Paul in the New: to answer when they were called; to go where they were sent. So Susa was not merely a new place for them to live; they were already on a missionary journey, the same mission which to this day remains the vocation of the Daughters of St Paul. It is a task which will never be completed. Teresa Merlo reflected on all this and made it a part of herself; in particular she grew to know and understand what it meant to obey. She achieved a mastery of this virtue, not simply as an obligation, a restriction, or an escape from responsibility, but as her reply to an invitation from God. It was an obedience which sometimes called for her to lower her eyes, but never to close them.

Fr Alberione also brought regular news of Alba to the community at Susa. This was particularly important because there had been rumours that he had received attractive invitations to move from Piedmont; for example the influential Cardinal Archbishop of Pisa, Pietro Maffi, would have liked to take him to work in his diocese.

James Alberione certainly had plenty of difficulties to contend with at Alba. His opponents within the Church had not given up the fight; and on the political front the anticlerical faction was still making itself heard, though this was more a matter of noise rather than of substance. The girls at Susa would not have known much about this, for it was not Alberione's way to dramatise his troubles; on the contrary, he did his utmost to hide them from others. And so in due course, without referring to his tribulations, he was able to announce that a group of young women at Alba, led by Angela Raballo, had been able to keep the Printing School in operation, and that the number of new recruits was growing.

The year 1919 drew to a gratifying conclusion with the ordination to the priesthood in October of the first of Fr Alberione's young men, the same Giuseppe Giaccardo that he had discovered as a twelve-year-old boy at Narzole.

The Pauline City

The summer of 1921 was a period of momentous developments. In the previous year Fr Alberione had bought just over 20 acres of agricultural land on the outskirts of Alba, flanked by broad highways on two sides and on the others by the Cherasca torrent and the Asti-Alessandria railway. On this site he commissioned a magnificent building of five stories. It was ready for occupation by August of the following year and the young men immediately moved in with their printing presses. This machinery was also new, thanks to an unusual stroke of good luck. At Sesto San Giovanni near Milan a business which specialised in pornographic and anti-clerical publications had gone into liquidation. Fr Alberione was among the first to hear about this and he immediately rushed over with a group of his boys. They quickly agreed a price, paid for the equipment, dismantled it, and moved it back to Alba. On 5 October of the same year the five young men who had taken vows in 1917 and eight other church students from the Alba seminary, together with Fr Alberione, adopted for the first time the name of the *Pia Società di San Paolo*, the Pious Society of St Paul, thus constituting themselves as a community officially distinct from the Printing School.

The new building was barely completed before Alberione recalled the contractors to double its size. Yet the resulting construction was to be only one part of the Pauline city which would later take shape among the pastures on the outskirts of Alba and which was eventually dominated by the imposing lines of the great church dedicated to the Apostle Paul.

In the summer of 1922 Bishop Re, who by now was fully

won over to the new enterprise, brought the priestly strength of the Society to four when on 29 June he ordained Giovanni Battista Ghione, Sebastiano Trosso and Angelo Fenoglio to join Fr Giaccardo.

A religious congregation takes shape

"I have always dreamed of a religious order which was also a publishing house." So wrote Cardinal Maffi in the historic autumn of 1921 in a letter to Fr Alberione, adding: "I said a very special prayer of thanks when I heard that you had undertaken this mission. And is it not a proof of heaven's blessing that you have received so much financial and material help?"

Whilst he acknowledged the role of part-time collaborators in spreading the Gospel through the printed word, the Cardinal, when he spoke of a religious publishing house, was underlining the special need for men and women who were prepared to make it a vocation for life.

The newly formed Society of St Paul now needed official recognition by Bishop Re as an institute of diocesan right, but before that could happen the Congregation of Religious in Rome had to study all the documents and give its approval. Fr Alberione made a personal journey to the Vatican to follow the procedure from close at hand and he was granted a private audience with Pope Benedict XV during the early days of 1922. James Alberione was one of the last people to be received by him, for he died on 22 January. Shortly afterwards, with the new Pope Pius XI (Ratti) on the throne of Peter, the Congregation rejected the request for recognition. The Curia was not yet ready to acknowledge the need for a new religious family. There was still a long way to go. Undeterred, Fr Alberione set in motion the procedure for the recognition of the women's community.

During the evenings at Susa, when the thoughts of Teresa and her companions took them back to Alba, they remembered everything on the minute scale of the early days – the tiny rooms, the workshops where they had sat huddled together for lack of space, that small group of girls hidden from the world. After such deprivations, every new report from home seemed like an incredible victory against the odds. So it was in festive mood that they set out for Alba for a few days' visit, to see their families, to make a retreat, to admire the new premises, and to savour the achievements of their colleagues.

After the retreat some of the younger members of the community made their first private vows. Later, on 22 July, Fr Alberione assembled the older ones for a ceremony in which they made their private religious profession, undertaking to devote the whole of their lives to the new apostolate in these words: "Binding ourselves together with the bonds of charity at the end of our spiritual exercises, and committing ourselves to the vows of chastity, obedience, poverty and loyalty to the Pope, we undertake to devote the whole of our lives to 'the good press' and to live the life of our divine Master, seeing with the eyes of Mary, Queen of Apostles, and inspired by the guidance of the Apostle Paul."

This was the true moment of birth of the community of the Daughters of St Paul with just nine original members, each adopting a new name in religion: Eufrosina Binello (Margherita Maria), Angela Boffi (Paolina Maria), Maria Carbone (Caterina Maria), Giuseppina Cordero (Francesca Maria), Annunziata Manera (Agnese Maria), Teresa Merlo (Thecla Maria), Angela Raballo (Teresa Maria), Elena Rinaldi (Paola Maria), Maria Soldano (Edvige Maria).

As well as the nine professed sisters, there were four novices and 15 postulants, 28 in all. None of them was able yet to wear the religious habit; that would come later; there was no hurry. The nine sisters had taken the same vows as their male brethren, including the fourth one, of special loyalty to the Pope. Fr Alberione had decided on this after careful consideration. He had to bear in mind the new and singular character of the Institute, which needed a firm anchorage in the See of Rome; and he was also mindful of the times, still troubled by both the disruptive activities of the Modernists and the excessive zeal of their opponents.

In fact Modernism did not inflict anything like as much damage on the diocese of Alba as elsewhere. This was not because it was suppressed with greater vigour, but because Bishop Re and Canon Chiesa, by insisting on sound religious instruction in the seminary, already commanded the ground in which this error took root elsewhere. In these circumstances James Alberione – precisely because he was embarking on an entirely new interpretation of the apostolate – wanted his intentions to be clearly spelt out and all his actions to be guided by one simple principle, which he called *Romanità* – complete faithfulness to the teachings of the Holy See, which he referred to as their "fundamental resource". The fourth vow, adopted by the Paulines on their own initiative, was a consequence of this. They were proclaiming their total loyalty in all their work to the authority of the Pope, placing themselves visibly at the service of the Church and of its head.

Maestra Thecla, Superior General

But that was not all that happened on 22 July 1922. In the afternoon Fr Alberione called together the whole female community. In effect this was a kind of general chapter, especially solemn because it was the first. On this occasion history was not made in surroundings of frescoed walls and Gothic vaults. The community met in the more informal atmosphere of the kitchen, among the pots and pans. Alberione again emphasised the significance of the step they had taken that morning, and then he continued with these words: "You will not be called "Sister" or "Mother" but "Maestra"; and not only to honour the divine Master, but also because you must follow his example, acting as a light and a guide to the souls who will be entrusted to you. By your presence among ordinary people and by your works you must represent Jesus Christ, the Way the Truth and the Life."

Teresa Merlo, now Maestra Thecla, was excited and moved – as were they all – by these words, which summoned women from the support battalions into the front line of evangelisation. But the final words of Fr Alberione, the Founder, stunned them all: "From this moment your Superior General will be Maestra Thecla. I am electing her for twelve years. After that you can arrange matters for yourselves."

That July day had already been a sufficiently memorable one for her, for the other young women, and for the future of the whole venture before Fr Alberione unveiled that final surprise – and without even asking for her acceptance or agreement. She had no reason to expect anything more. In the morning she had taken the name of Thecla, a disciple of St Paul, an attractive character from the story of the early church, who listened secretly to the apostle at Iconium in Asia Minor, a handmaid of the living God, a preacher of the Gospel, a woman caught up in great events. Teresa Merlo, having adopted the same name and finding herself immediately afterwards appointed Superior, had become another handmaid of the living God, a latter-day collaborator of St Paul. Yet her reaction was one of profound simplicity. She is not recorded as having uttered a single memorable word on that astonishing occasion, nor even when it was spoken about later. No speeches, no tears, no excitement; her acceptance was humble and brief. If God willed it so, he would surely support her in the task.

With his short talk among the pots and pans on 22 July 1922, Fr Alberione quickly disposed of the problem of managing the new religious family. Less easily solved was the problem of governing Italy, which had collapsed during that summer into total disorder. In many places Fascists were taking over the functions of the State without the slightest legal warrant, whilst government ministers found themselves powerless to exercise their authority. Most notably powerless among the politicians was the Prime Minister himself, Luigi Facta from Pinerolo in Piedmont, a prisoner of the rival groups which made up the parliamentary majority. He was forced to resign. On this, Senator Alfredo Frassati wrote to Alfredo Giolitti: "In its hour of need Italy has turned unanimously to you. You can no longer be simply the head of a faction; we need a leader of the country in the battle of ideas which is upon us." Giolitti, a man of eighty, had already headed five governments. When he refused a sixth term as premier he probably made it easier for the 39-year-old Mussolini to claim for himself the title of *Duce*, "leader of the nation".

Fr Alberione himself gave no particular prominence to Thecla's appointment. Years afterwards, recalling her early days, he painted a very down-to-earth picture of her: "She was a sickly young woman with a delicate constitution. But the Lord works in his own ways. We must always remember that holiness is ultimately rooted in action, in a life which is wise and yet human. First come the natural virtues, and then those with a social dimension, which are learned in the family. On this basis we build the Christian virtues under the guidance of true religion." James Alberione was never fond of elaborate displays of devotion; before all else he prized "a life which is wise and yet human".

On another occasion he gave this account of her: "Hearing God's call at about 20 years of age, she joined the small group of young girls who were preparing to become, in due course, the Daughters of St Paul. She did not enjoy good health, and I doubted whether she would be able to stay the course, for her fragile constitution was soon in evidence. However the good Lord came to her rescue, and to such effect that with the help of his grace – and by her own determination and prudent manner of life – she lived to be seventy."

When Fr Alberione announced that Thecla Merlo was to be Superior General, several of the young women around her in the kitchen were surprised and upset. Most of them had regarded Angela Maria Boffi as the natural candidate because of her age, her qualifications, and her dedication to the apostolate. Others considered her too severe, though none could fail to admire her simplicity of life nor the passion that she put into her work, especially at Susa. She had always worked well with Thecla. But her enormous energy and impatience for results had led her into some rather speculative personal ventures, and one purchase of land had given rise to unpleasantness. The matter was quietly settled without serious consequences, but Fr Alberione became convinced that Angela Maria Boffi, whom he continued to hold in high esteem, was destined for other things.

Later in 1922, still on the best of terms with everyone, she left the Daughters to return to Susa, where she spent a short period as a member of the Franciscan Tertiaries, founded by a future Blessed, Bishop Eduardo Rosaz. Then early in 1926 it seemed that she could at last fulfil her long-cherished wish to enter an enclosed order, when she was accepted by the Little Sisters of St Francis da Paola at Marseilles.

But fate denied her once again. After a short time she was stricken with a fatal illness and left the monastery to spend her last days with relatives at Nove Ligure, her birthplace in the Province of Alessandria. On 26 October 1926 Angela Maria Boffi, Maestra Paolina in her days among the Daughters of St Paul, died following an operation. She was barely 40.

Though Angela's departure from the Pauline family had been entirely amicable, her death came as a painful blow to Thecla. Despite the differences in age and temperament they had always understood one another, sharing their burdens and hopes like sisters. Both of them had offered a model and an inspiration to the others.

Another great inspiration was Canon Chiesa. The advice of this singularly influential man was sought and followed at many decisive stages in the evolution of the Congregation. His was the stuff that great bishops are made of, yet he was content to remain in charge of a parish at Alba for most of his priestly life. It was no gesture of renunciation on his part, but the conscious choice of a man whose only wish was to be in the front line with clearly defined responsibilities that he could embrace with enthusiasm. Fr Alberione would often speak of those who carried these responsibilities as "the hidden foundations", referring to the invisible structures that hold up the weight of houses, churches, palaces and towers. Francesco Chiesa was undoubtedly one of these – a man of learning, of exemplary life, with a gift for plain words and deeply versed in the arts of spiritual guidance.

After being appointed Prima Maestra Thecla Merlo lost no time in consulting Canon Chiesa on a question which she had not dared to put to Fr Alberione (and even less to her parish priest at Castagnito, Fr Pistone). She was anxious to know whether her nomination truly represented the will of God, and whether her acceptance of it had been an act of true obedience or a disguised surrender to vanity.

Francesco Chiesa knew both her and James Alberione too well to have any doubts. His answer was clear and certain: "It is Our Lord himself who wants this. Have no fear, Thecla. You will be the one who writes this story; or rather you will be one of many writers. You are moving into uncharted waters, because Fr Alberione has in mind something that has never before been heard of. What he wants to create is not two separate religious families – one for men, one for women – but something quite unique, with the two parts working side by side like regiments in an infantry division. He will be the overall head. You will of course be the Superior General of the Daughters, though subject to an even more General Superior, the Theologian."

However Alberione was asking rather too much. Even the more sympathetic of the Roman prelates were taken aback by such a proposal, and the business became so drawn out that Pope Pius XI had to intervene personally. Meanwhile Maestra Thecla found herself having to act as

Superior General in circumstances which were, to say the least, unusual. Later in life, when she used to say to the Daughters of St Paul that "the cross ought not to be dragged but carried", she knew what she was talking about.

In October 1922, whilst Mussolini marched on Rome and the Fascists occupied the local town hall, the Daughters of St Paul were settling into the new headquarters of the Society at Alba. They were not yet at their final destination. They were later to move within the same complex into what was called the House of Divine Providence, and it was not until 1933 that they finally came to occupy a new home which was completely their own. It stands in what was traditionally known as the San Cassiano district, near the road from Alba to Pollenzo, taking its name from an Irish martyr who suffered death there in the year 311 along with the Gaul Frontiniano. After the first World War the area was renamed Borgo Piave.

Maestra Thecla returned to Susa to supervise the hand-over of the printing activities and the book shop. *La Valsusa*, whose revival had been decreed by Bishop Castelli and secured by the energies of the Daughters, was now on a firm footing; so on 23 March 1923 Thecla and her companions finally left Susa to join the other Daughters at Alba. The fusion was not achieved without problems. The early experiences of the two groups had been quite different, and though everyone had had to work extremely hard, many felt that they borne heavier burdens than others. Maestra Thecla gradually overcame these problems, preserving discipline whilst avoiding the needless humiliations which at that time were common practice in some of the older religious orders.

The Pact with Our Lord

So in 1923 Fr Alberione had again gathered all his forces around him at Alba. At this stage, as well as almost 200 members of the male Institute, there were about 50 Daughters and postulants in the female community. People began to take notice of the unaccustomed buzz of activity centred on the buildings which had so recently risen among the meadows at the edge of the city, with the comings and goings of so many young men and women – the priests and seminarians usually wearing cassocks, the rest in normal clothes. They were treated with a rather ambiguous tolerance: on the one hand, they enjoyed the personal protection of the bishop; on the other, they lacked any sort of formal recognition, even at diocesan level.

The people of Alba had no real notion of what was taking shape in their midst, less still of what it would later become. But one thing at least was very evident: the young people of this community, right down to its most junior members, worked extremely hard and for long hours. James Alberione had not yet convinced the doubters, let alone won over his opponents. But it was clear to everyone about him, from the newest recruit to the ordained priest – even to the returning war veteran Captain Sebastiano Trosso – that he was utterly determined to drive forward.

The presses never ceased to turn and there was a constant traffic of deliveries by hand-cart to and from the railway station. Fr Alberione boasted confidently that it would not always be so: "One day, you'll see, the train will come here to collect the newspapers and books from us." The trains did indeed come and he lived to see his prophecy fulfilled.

Among their first titles was *Vita pastorale* (Pastoral life), a monthly which went out to every parish in Italy, and was particularly valued for the help it gave to priests, bringing them up-to-date with all manner of new ideas. It also ensured that the other activities of the Society of St Paul became known throughout the country. In 1923 they introduced *La Domenica* (Sunday) and *La buona parola* (The good word); these were lively weekly Mass sheets aimed at a lay readership, but they were also helpful to the clergy in their pastoral work. The first enabled ordinary people to follow the Latin Mass, whilst the second provided background reading to accompany religious instruction. Shortly afterwards they launched *Giornalino* (Small daily), preparing children for spiritual growth through their lives, and *L'Aspirante* (The aspirant), aimed at the younger members of Catholic Action.

Later still came books, parish bulletins, pamphlets campaigning against bad language… the work was interminable, the pressure unremitting. The Daughters were chiefly involved with the books – correcting proofs, stitching leaflets, making and stacking a never-ending flow of packages, handling literally tons of paper every day. Fr Alberione was regularly in attendance to check every detail down to the last fold. "Who could have better reason than you to make sure that we send out books that are beautifully made?" he would ask. His stern methods called for every moment of the day to be usefully occupied. For him this was the only way to achieve what they all hoped for and desired; and he was as hard on himself as he was on others, both on the worldly and the supernatural level. Their task was to earn their keep by their own efforts, to spread the Gospel, and to save souls – starting with their own. He was quite prepared to put his own health at risk and he expected the same dedication from them all, without exception. The only concession he would allow was the one in the old saying: you could take a rest by changing jobs.

Fr Giaccardo left this note about Alberione's demands on his followers: "Father explained how he expected us to study at the house: to give only half our time to it, and yet learn at twice the speed. In other words, when we had one hour to study we had to learn as much as others would in four. He had made a pact with Our Lord: the young people of "the good press" would never complete their education with study alone; they also had to work. But for this apostolate they needed to know much more than ordinary priests. So on the one hand the Theologian made sure that we worked and prayed, whilst on the other, the good Lord promised that we should learn at four times the speed. This applied not just to our study but to the whole of life. It called for a great deal of faith at first, but the Theologian made sure that everyone in the house accepted it. Anyone who fell by the wayside did so for lack of faith. Each of us had to be worth four ordinary people. Anyone who was unwilling to accept this – who lacked this faith – was told to go somewhere else where they could afford four hours of study to produce four hours of learning." In the history of the Society this has become known as the "the Pact, or the Secret of Success" – a contract between Fr Alberione and Our Lord.

Maestra Thecla had to learn the Founder's method of working, observing his Pact and at the same time bringing all the Daughters to the same level of dedication. That remarkable contract between heaven and earth had already been shown to work in her own case when she arrived from Castagnito, and many times since. Alberione himself wrote of this in 1954: "Teresa put herself to bed almost as soon as she arrived, yet she had already struck those present with a quality which commanded respect – almost reverence. It was then that we gave the undertaking to Our Lord which is contained in our Pact, or Secret of Success, and which has come to our help in our greatest trials and needs." Some were disheartened, "but the Pact was being continually renewed. And everything combined to show that Our Lord works behind the scenes, though with great effect, and that ordinary goodness allied with common sense often produces better results than physical strength and technical skill."

The preparation of the Daughters for their mission was fraught with difficulties. Nowhere else in the world of consecrated women was anything of the kind being attempted; nowhere else was so much being demanded. Indeed some families began to have serious misgivings about the enterprise. They were far from happy to hear that the daughters they had entrusted to Fr Alberione were not being provided with a proper habit like other sisters, and were being kept hard at work for long hours. It even happened on one occasion whilst he was giving a homily to the community that the parents of one girl burst in to take their daughter home.

Thecla stood at the very centre of this task of selection and formation, but though she acted under the guidance of the Founder she was also humbly aware that some of his principles needed to be translated into a female idiom. In order to achieve the substance of what he required she had to adopt a more appropriate form and style. To be sure, she never allowed herself to modify or soften the essential severity of the Pauline rule as it evolved; for her, everything that fell from the lips of the Primo Maestro was quite simply the word of God. But she needed to help her young women to understand and to love that word.

Those who had been tempered in this regime did not find it too difficult to summon the enterprise and courage needed for their pioneering forays, without material or moral support, to the other side of the world. After the experience of Alba they would not be intimidated by any later fear or discouragement.

It must also be added that James Alberione was helped by the times and local culture that he worked in, and it is to his credit that he well understood this. He discovered and selected his men and women – so rich with the spirit of self-sacrifice, and later, of enterprise – among the surrounding hills, getting to know the hamlets, the farmsteads, the country parishes, and seeing how their families lived. He weighed his choices by looking squarely into the eyes of the fathers and mothers who trudged down to Alba on foot or in the farm buggy. (He himself had first arrived at the seminary riding on an ox-cart.) He could almost say he knew some of the young people before he met them. It was enough for him to know where they came from to guess what sort of family it was, how the children were brought up, the kind of life they led. He had such an intimate knowledge of the area that it was almost impossible for him to make a bad choice.

Nevertheless, to have conceived, launched and developed these two communities in the face of misunderstanding, distrust and obstruction remains an almost miraculous achievement. These young people were required to give themselves up to a life of both prayer and sheer drudgery. They spent their days with books which occupied their minds as students and their hands as labourers. Later they acquired even more improbable skills as need arose – the baking and laying of bricks for the construction of their buildings, paper-making to feed the appetite of their presses, bread-making and cookery for the support of the community. On top of this, men and women together, they had to master religious doctrine and the principles of accountancy. And everything was accompanied by long and fervent prayer, in which the Primo Maestro set the example by spending three or four hours every day on his knees.

As if these were not burdens enough, the Pauline family had to make other sacrifices, which were felt most particularly by the women. They were not allowed two of the customary consolations of the religious life – the name of an illustrious and esteemed congregation and the habit. The habit was particularly missed, for in those days it was the distinguishing mark which proclaimed and confirmed a sister's vocation; and the joyful wearing of it, in public and at solemn observances, was a gratifying symbol of collective identity.

These women had no such satisfactions. Thecla was the first to venture forth, and she later led others by the hand down the highways and byways as they went about the business of their unprecedented calling. Alberione was also there to reassure them. For him this was not uncharted territory; these were highways and byways that he had trodden in earlier days, the scenes of battles already won.

He often spoke of his own pioneer predecessors, and it was through him that Thecla came to learn about Alfonso Rodriguez, a worldly Spanish merchant of the late 15th and early 16th century, who lost wife and children at the age of 42. It was a misfortune that shook him to the foundations and brought him down to earth. He cast himself in the humblest of roles, acting for 34 years as door-keeper of the Jesuit house in Palma, Majorca. "Here is a man to follow", said Alberione. "God gave that door-keeper exceptional wisdom. His advice was eagerly sought, and at the urging of his superiors he wrote several books of piety and devotion. The Church made him a Saint, and Our Lord, who grants wisdom to those who seek it, made him an example of his generosity."

Then there was Jean Marie Vianney, the curé of Ars, who died in 1859 and was much discussed at that time. Thecla knew that Pope Pius XI was on the point of proclaiming this holy man a Saint – it would happen in 1925 – but she learned from Alberione that this patron of parish priests had been sent home from the seminary because he was not considered clever enough. Among the subjects that he could not master was Latin, so he undertook a lengthy pilgrimage on foot to a mountain sanctuary to pray for the grace to learn it. And learn it he did.

Alberione insisted repeatedly that nothing comes easily, but that everything was possible at Alba under the patronage of St Paul: the wisdom of Rodriguez, the Latin of the Curé d'Ars and the pact by which "one yields four". Holiness could also be won in this day and age: in chapel, among the printing presses, in the stock rooms, the laundry, the school or at catechism with Canon Chiesa. And as long as he lived, the Founder never tired of saying that he needed "holy women who are hidden from the eyes of the world, who are seen only by God. Such women will indeed build the Kingdom."

So this was Maestra Thecla's task: to mould herself for her great vocation and the other young women after her. There was no time to work out precise methods of instruction; she simply carried on with her daily duties, learning and teaching as she did so. But could she, with her uncertain health, manage all this? Often her humble spirit must have asked the question. Could she really act as teacher, model and guide, now that she had begun to realise her own academic deficiencies? She must have pondered many times on the evidence to the contrary. The dreams of her youth had been about quite humdrum accomplishments: to be a competent seamstress, a worthy nun, a good catechist for Fr Pistone at Castagnito. She had ample reason to wonder if she was cut out to shoulder responsibilities of a totally different order.

She was not the sort who made a great display of her spiritual difficulties. Only once at the beginning of her term as Superior General did she go down on her knees in public to accuse herself of lack of dedication. The gesture was not well received and she never repeated it. Canon Chiesa gave her great encouragement, and indeed her natural common sense helped her to build and strengthen her own morale. She had never wanted the position of Prima Maestra; she accepted it only because it was the wish of Fr Alberione. But she could not let him down now. For his part he was keeping all his promises: new houses, presses, newspapers, books and vocations. There seemed no choice but to obey, especially when he was always saying there was so much more to be done.

When he said they could do a thing it was useless to plead lack of means or qualifications. Some remarks he made in May 1928 are typical of his reaction to negative attitudes: "Our vocation takes a novel form, and the good Lord has shown us a special favour by enlisting us for this work. Which of us ever dreamed of such a calling? He has taken us – ignorant, clumsy and ungifted that we are – from our various occupations, as he did the apostles, and he has called us to a task which is of service to every other vocation, namely the apostolate of the press. We who are the first in the field will have the greater merit if we do our work well – and the greater responsibility if we fail."

So there was never any question of refusing any job they were given, even when they might be "ignorant, clumsy and ungifted". They had nothing like Canon Chiesa's three university degrees or Fr Trosso's officer training. Yet, despite their modest school backgrounds, the Daughters knew there was always a way, the way of the Curé of Ars, whose Latin had been judged first "weak" and then later "extremely weak", and who had nevertheless gone on to become one of the greatest priests in the history of the Church.

Perseverance in times of difficulty

Let us take a look at Maestra Thecla at work during these years when she was developing her own character and that of the Daughters. We have already seen her humanity and respect for others and the way this enabled her to offer gentle encouragement to those in difficulty. But that was by no means the whole of her.

Here in her own words is a rebuke she gave to the Daughters when they were showing signs of flagging: "We should be the strength and the driving force of the house; it's up to us to set an example of boundless energy and enthusiasm in all our activities. Yet here we are, resigning ourselves, losing our grip and our passion, without considering the seriousness of the account we must render to Our Lord. We have made our vows; we have all consecrated ourselves to God; but we haven't yet given up our self-will, for we still see cases of reluctant obedience, loss of temper and careless work. We lack that extra eagerness. And short-lived enthusiasm isn't enough; we need something that lasts, that doesn't let us down in the face of difficulties. So let's think seriously about this! It is a matter of the greatest importance for our own souls and for the good of the house, bearing in mind that each of us is in contact with the others and everything that one of us does affects the rest."

Here we have some flavour of her style of group leadership. But personal formation was an individual matter: one case at a time, face to face, in a supportive spirit and with full discussion and explanations. Sometimes one of the Daughters would share a problem with her in confidence; perhaps she had not been able to understand some order from the Primo Maestro. On such occasions Thecla was both sisterly and firm: "You know, there are many times when I too don't understand, or even disagree, when the Primo Maestro tells me to do something, and I often want to tell him so. But then I pause and think, if the Primo Maestro wants it so, that's a sure sign that it will be all right, that it must be that way. And after a while I realise that he was right, that it was a good thing that we did as we were told. It invariably turns out for the best."

But in spite of the dedication of all concerned it seemed, in the summer of 1923, that the Society of St Paul was about to collapse. For some time Fr Alberione had been suffering from pains in the throat and was eating less and less. On 13 July his mother died, but he still carried on with his unremitting daily routine. Then one evening, returning from preaching, he collapsed. Three doctors were called in turn, but their verdict was unanimous: he was suffering from tuberculosis, and at best he could expect only another eighteen months of life.

He was taken to Benevello, a village in the hills standing at just over 2,000 feet and overlooking the valleys of the Cherasca and the Belbo, where the parish priest, Fr Brovia, was his great friend. He was given a quiet room in the presbytery, and arrangements were made for his nursing. The moment of crisis passed, and little by little he found the will to fight back. His weakness was extreme: he was even unable to hold a book in his hands. He had someone read to him from the *Spiritual exercises* of St Ignatius Loyola, the "knight of God", who set down his first principles four hundred years ago at Manresa following a strange experience as he watched the waters of the river Cardoner rushing past him: "As I was sitting there, the eyes of my mind suddenly began to open. It wasn't that I was seeing a vision, but from that moment I knew and understood many things about the spiritual life, about the Faith and about the printed word..."

How often must James Alberione have asked himself, as he lay there pondering the doctors' verdict, what all those young people would do if he failed to recover? The work was scarcely begun; heavy debts had been incurred. Perhaps he considered possible candidates to succeed him. Perhaps he meditated, in his sickness and worry, on St Ignatius' advice in moments of crisis: "Take care never to make changes in the hour of your desolation, but rather stay firm and constant in the decisions you made and the intentions you formed in earlier moments of calm..." In due course a combination of good nursing, the climate of Benevello and Fr Brovia's hospitality helped him towards recovery and by September, though still not completely cured, he was able to return to Alba. The doctors revised their estimate of his chances of survival by some tens of years, though there were momentary fears of a relapse when he fainted during Mass on Christmas Day.

It was a false alarm. He gradually recovered most of his former vigour, apart from a predisposition to arthritis and occasional brief bouts of illness, for which Fr Giaccardo gave this explanation: "Father normally enjoys excellent health, but any act of disobedience or other misdemeanour in the house gives him such stomach cramps that he can't digest his food; so by watching his ups and downs we know whether we have a sinner among us."

He had to watch carefully throughout 1924 for signs of a return of the tuberculosis and he was often confined to his bed. On those occasions one of his most assiduous nurses was Thecla herself: "During 1924 he got gradually better, though he was often confined to his bed. As one of the senior members of the community I regularly went to look after him."

It seems that he came to a new decision during the bleak days at Benevello, though its roots ran deep and far into the past. On 21 November 1923 he announced to the women's

*Castagnito d'Alba, the birthplace of Teresa Merlo, future
Co-foundress of the Congregation of the Daughters of St Paul.*

*Teresa's parents,
Vicenza and
Ettore Merlo.*

*The cot which was
used for Teresa
and all the Merlo
children.*

Below: *Teresa's
room.*

The house where Teresa was born. It was restored in 1989 as a house of prayer and contains an exhibition illustrating the life of Maestra Thecla and the history of the Congregation.

Below: *Teresa with her brothers and their families.*

A family group of 1914.
Teresa stands with her brothers
John (centre) and Costanzo,
who was already studying for
the priesthood. Her youngest
brother, Carlo sits at the front.
In the centre row (from right)
are her father, her paternal
grandfather, Giovanni Battista,
her mother and her mother's
sister.

Right: *Teresa at the age*
of 20, a detail from the
photograph opposite.

Left: *James Alberione at 53. He first met Teresa in 1915 and invited her to collaborate with him in a venture which was to prove historic and prophetic.*

Below: *The front page of an early edition of* La Valsusa. *This diocesan weekly was printed by the future Daughters of St Paul from January 1919 until March 1923.*

Right: *The group at Susa in 1922. Angela Maria Boffi (front row, second from left) was then the manageress and Teresa (front row, right) her assistant.*

The first nine members of the community, who on 22 July 1922 took vows, dedicating themselves to the apostolate of "the good press". Teresa took the name Thecla and was appointed Superior General.

Standing from left: *Agnese Manera, Edvige Soldano, Margherita Binello, Francesca Cordero, Caterina Carbone, Paola Rinaldi.* *Seated: Teresa Merlo, Teresa Raballo, Paolina Boffi.*

Alba 1923: Novices in the warehouse prepare books for despatch.

Alba 1933: Sisters and novices at work in the binding department.

Below: *Fr. Alberione and Maestra Thecla at the Boston Book Centre
in 1955. Sister Paula Cordero presents the Founder with a 16mm
film whilst Sister Sabina Meneghelli shows Maestra Thecla some of
the new titles published by the Daughters in the USA.*

Left: *Rome 15 October 1952: Mgr Montini, then Pro Secretary of State, pays a visit to the Pauline family in Rome to bring the blessing of Pope Pius XII on their catechetical film enterprise. He is seen here with Fr Alberione and Maestra Thecla at the Generalate.*

Right: *A portrait of Maestra Thecla from the late 1950's.*

From left: *Maestra Redenta Commentucci, Maestra Thecla,
Fr James Alberione and Sister Laurentia Casamassima
during the first visit to Sydney in May 1955.*

*Rome 4 May 1957: The participants
at the first General Chapter.
The three General Councillors are in
the front row: Maestra Nazarena
Morando next to Maestra Thecla and
Maestra Ignazia Balla and Maestra
Amalia Peyrolo to Fr. Alberione's left*

1960: Maestra Thecla arrives at Valencia (Spain) accompanied by Sr. Lucia Monterumici.

community that two of the Daughters, Orsolina Rivata and Metilde Gerlotto, were to be detached from the rest. As he explained: "We have set Orsolina and Metilde aside in order to create a family dedicated to prayer." Later he was to take another six from Maestra Thecla, and with these eight a separate community was born, dedicated to the special calling of perpetual adoration, in which they took turns to watch and pray before the tabernacle. In addition, they were to attend to the household arrangements for the whole Pauline family; they were to be seen doing the washing in the river Cherasca in all weathers. And everything, their prayers and the various domestic duties, were to be offered for the specific intentions of the house, especially for vocations and for the sanctification of the ordained and professed members of the community.

Alberione had spoken of this idea several years earlier to Canon Chiesa, who had encouraged him to set up this separate activity as soon as possible. The new family was officially constituted on 10 February 1924, the memorial of St Scholastica, with Orsolina Rivata as superior – Mother Mary Scholastica in religion. These sisters were also given their own special name, the Pious Disciples of the Divine Master. Moreover they were to have the habit, though this served an essentially liturgical function since it was worn only during the time that they spent before the tabernacle. This was a personal initiative of Fr Alberione, and he himself chose the colours. For this was not simply a matter of appearances: the visible aspects of perpetual adoration were an essential, if silent, contribution to the act of worship. He gave his personal attention to all aspects of the organisation of the *Pie Discepole*, their spiritual formation, rules, hours and accommodation. He attended to literally everything himself.

Maestra Thecla took no active part in this first stage, though Alberione did tell her about his decision one day in 1924 whilst she was nursing him. "I have decided to set up a group of Daughters with a special vocation to prayer," he said. It should be borne in mind that she had only returned to Alba in March 1923 and that memories of Susa were still fresh in her mind. Now she was gaining her first experiences of a new life, which was complicated by the endless problems posed by growing into her role in the community.

She realised of course that the Primo Maestro was the mind and heart of the enterprise; she knew it and accepted that it had to be so. But living beside him was always hard and sometimes painful. In the midst of her tribulations she must have thought from time to time of the Curé of Ars. She may have reflected that some of his achievements – the long road to ordination and his painful experience of the world of books – were not perhaps as superhuman as she had thought, considering her own tribulations on the way to becoming a good Daughter and a good teacher.

In the early days she was often distressed by the looks of bewilderment and even dismay among the Daughters when they received their instructions. Yet no cloud ever seemed to cross her face; she was always able to maintain the untroubled expression typical of the Merlo family. She invariably responded with silent, unquestioning and immediate obedience to Fr Alberione's orders, keeping firmly to herself all feelings of resentment and temptations to resist. Her obedience led her to accept an active share in the later arrangements for the Pious Disciples though it was Alberione who selected the Daughters to be transferred – and with few concessions to tact or fine feelings.

Such were the methods of a man whose mind was permanently focused on the challenges of the future rather than immediate difficulties. Many found it impossible to work with such a person, but not Thecla. Indeed she not only survived, but carried on her life and performed her duties without ever losing her composure in the highly charged atmosphere which surrounded this volcanic character, who by now had ample confirmation of her determination and powers of endurance.

Alberione knew that the little seamstress from Castagnito

had come a long way since, in his words, "she opened up her mind and heart towards the souls of others" at Canon Chiesa's school. He knew that he could count on her support in the work of his new foundations, and in 1954, when their early problems lay in the distant past, he was happy to acknowledge her role. "She was unfailingly helpful to me in the spiritual formation of the Daughters of St Paul, in guiding their steps along the path of their specific mission, in resolving the thornier problems of the early years – and there were many – and in setting up the Pious Disciples and the Sisters of Jesus the Good Shepherd, also known as the *Pastorelle*. I received invaluable support from her in bringing both these Congregations into being, in helping them to develope and in obtaining official approval for their Constitutions. She later advised and supported them, both morally and financially, often at considerable sacrifice to herself. Both these families honour her and are deeply in her debt."

Chapter Three

AT THE SERVICE
OF THE GOSPEL

The year 1924 witnessed a beautifully simple episode in the Pauline story which greatly moved the whole community at the time. One evening the young men from the printing department carried some stacks of finished sheets into what was called "the room of the apostolate", passing the work on from one stage of production to the next, in which the Daughters were to perform the folding and stitching. But this was a different task from any they had undertaken before: for the first time they were handling the text of the Gospel. In the words of "Our Atlas", the history of the Daughters of St Paul, "The whole community gathered around those pages and each of the sisters kissed them reverently. But before starting their work they decided they must purify their souls in the sacrament of Penance and cleanse their hands in the manner of the priest before he touches the sacred host. From that time onwards the sacred Scriptures were exposed in every room, and the Gospel and the Bible were always held in special veneration." Fr Alberione was present on that occasion and he assured them that before long the Daughters of St Paul would have distributed the Scriptures in thousands and even millions of copies.

The Founder gradually adapted his original vision to the conditions and needs of the times; what was now needed was more than merely an embattled community of writers, lecturers and publishers. The ideological conflicts which had inflamed the early years of the century, many of them reflecting specifically Italian concerns, were becoming increasingly irrelevant.

The political climate had changed, but there still remained that deep ignorance of religious matters which had inspired the encyclicals of Pius X, and which caused him such pain to the end of his life. Alberione's objectives now implied a fully international operation devoted to the spread of the Word of God and the teaching of the Church, an operation that would leap frontiers and exploit the most up-to-date methods – the fastest and most efficient, as the Founder would repeatedly stress. He was beginning to formulate a concrete answer to the problem of "what to do for the men and women of the twentieth century", the challenge he had first become aware of on that night of 31 December 1900.

That gesture of the Daughters as they gathered round the newly printed verses of the Gospel, that feeling of a need for preparation – even a sacramental preparation – for their new work, recalls both the eucharistic liturgy and, from a more remote past, the reverent love of ancient Israel for the Divine Word recorded in the Law. Indeed to the uninitiated eye the actions of that evening might seem almost like the taking of another vow, a self-giving confirmed through the unique eloquence of ritual, as though to express an offering of themselves to the Gospel for the whole of their lives.

In the talks he gave to the Daughters Alberione always insisted that the prime purpose of anyone who embraced the religious life was to make themselves holy, adding that holiness must inevitably start with the Gospel. Thecla summarised the Founder's precepts for herself and for her Daughters like this: "No book of ours ought to be more frequently read than the one given to us by the Church." And again in tones that recall the Old Testament: "The Gospel is the only book you should kiss. The priest kisses it at the altar; let it always be in your mind, on your lips and in your heart. We do not seek to imitate the life of this Saint or that, only the Life of Jesus Christ himself."

So the Gospel was to be the key to their personal sanctification and their commitment as a community. It was this Gospel that they now had the task of taking to others. In the case of the Daughters 'to take' meant quite literally to carry. They did not wait for people in their book centres or outside churches; they went to look for them in the towns and on their doorsteps, in the market squares and at the cross-roads, out of doors and in their own homes.

Educator of apostles

The council of the women's Congregation, consisting of Fr Alberione, Maestra Thecla and the four sister Councillors, met in January 1925, and the minutes record an important new development. The Founder "drew the Maestra's attention to certain difficulties which were being experienced in the binding shop and in various other departments." When problems arose it had been Fr Alberione who decided how to resolve them. Now there was a new disposition. "From now on," we find recorded in the minutes, "Maestra Thecla was to oversee the management and direction of everything... Whereas previously Fr Alberione had sole charge of the running of the house, he would now become a Councillor so that any questions referred to him were to be taken as referring to her. Although Maestra Thecla would not have any particular title, she was to oversee matters of a general nature."

Today we might see a move of this kind as a reorganisation of management, with Thecla being promoted to the top position. But she herself saw the change in quite a different light; she saw the continuous spiritual formation of the sisters as her chief duty. Her notes, made during spiritual exercises and days of recollection, speak of her new managerial responsibilities as problems to be referred to the divine will and to the needs of the soul. "The cross is the high road to heaven. My Lenten penance will be to busy myself with administration." "It is God's will that I attend obediently to all these business matters." "Prepare myself for Easter; examine my conscience about problems of management."

Management problems certainly gave her plenty to think about. There was little that the other women's organisations in the Church were able to teach her, for no superior general in the world had yet had the task of forming a spirituality that struck a balance between prayer, study and heavy manual work. Among the problems not met in other communities were the tougher training and the need for stricter criteria of selection. Young girls, and even children, offered themselves as postulants often imagining the Daughters of St Paul to be quite different from what they actually were. Once they had seen the reality their reactions ranged from deep affection, through all the shades of feeling, to an intense dislike.

The records show that Thecla had various occasions to complain of "apathy at work, insufficient sense of urgency in completing important orders, disrespect towards superiors, slipping out of sight to avoid certain jobs, pretending to be mending their stockings rather than attending to the job they had been given."

It was because of this situation – not unusual in the early years of similar ventures – that Fr Alberione did not want to define Thecla's duties too precisely. Joining a religious congregation was sometimes seen as the quickest and least expensive way for a young girl to study for a teaching certificate; so not all of them enjoyed the long days of hard work, which were made still more burdensome by the discipline typical of a religious institution of its day. Those who joined the Congregation for the wrong reasons could not be expected to display the same singleness of mind and depth of faith that inspired the original devoted band and brought joy to their labours.

Thecla urged those in charge of the young ones to allow some latitude, at least in their spare time. This not only served to release pent-up energy, but also helped the sisters get to know their charges better as individuals. "In their recreation the girls are free to express themselves, to release their tensions; they become more themselves and are easier to know." This echoes the saying of Don Bosco, "A happy boy is an open book."

Alberione soon came to understand that Thecla Merlo was one of those uncommon people capable of forming the character of others whilst still working humbly to perfect their own. She would never neglect to correct a matter of detail, no matter how far below her notice as a religious superior it might seem. If she saw a girl folding pages clumsily she was not content simply to reprove her; she showed her how to do it herself, folding the paper again and again until the lesson was thoroughly learned. That was how she interpreted her duty of attending to management matters. And in school too, though she had such limited experience of conventional education, she showed herself enlightened in the matter of punishment. For example, instead of having the girls write the same sentence ten, twenty or thirty times – a dreadful imposition, which continued for many years even in lay schools – she would ask them to copy a story, so that at least they learned something from their penance.

But her gift as a spiritual guide did not consist of lowering standards so that even the lukewarm and the lazy could meet them. No, her standards remained firmly in place. Her way was to act on the motivation of her young women, making use of the special gifts of each and accepting all differences of character, providing they were compatible with well-directed growth. To quote from one of her circulars: "Education means cultivating the natural qualities and gifts of grace that a soul has already been given, so as to help it to become better and holier. To prepare girls for the religious life it isn't necessary to change every habit – only the bad ones. Nor is it necessary to repress all natural tendencies or to make everyone speak alike. What is needed is to instil the religious spirit, the life of faith and sacrifice, the love of God, of the apostolate and of all the means to sanctification. That is what really counts. Everything else is just ornament."

So the individuality of her postulants and nuns had to be treated with respect; they must not appear to have come out of a single mould. She tried to make each of them feel important with small demonstrations of personal attention – a letter, a card, a show of interest in the family. These methods also helped Thecla to play down the inevitable difficulties and dramas of growing up. By helping them to come to know themselves in peace of mind she pointed each along her own path, whether it lay within the community or led outside it.

Now we must look at another side of the Prima Maestra. We have seen her as the nun who prepared young women and small girls for the needs of the future. But at the same time, whilst everyone around her seemed to be worrying about money for printing machinery or to complete the construction of buildings, Thecla was asking some of her sisters to prepare themselves to move overseas – to Spain and Argentina – in the near future. And in early January 1926, she was telling others to be ready to go to Rome before the end of the month. The Pauline priests and brothers left first with Fr Giaccardo and the sisters followed immediately afterwards.

On their arrival they immediately came under the vigilant eye of the Roman Congregations, though without being recognised in any sense of that word. Indeed there was no basis for recognition as a religious institute since their very existence was still totally irregular. In the strictest sense, and speaking in the language of the Vatican, not even the Bishop of Alba recognised them. The day would come when the Sovereign Pontiffs themselves would be delighted to visit their houses in Rome, but for the moment these first representatives of the Pauline community had to slip timidly into the Eternal City like homeless wanderers or illegal immigrants.

Thereafter events moved quickly. Towards the end of January two small groups set out by train from Alba for Rome, bringing with them all they could manage to carry. One, the boys, was in the charge of Fr Giaccardo; the other, a group of Daughters, was led by Maestra Amalia Peyrolo.

Giaccardo and his party would later take delivery of the printing machinery and equipment, books, school benches and refectory tables. Provisional accommodation had been found for everyone by Fr Desiderio Costa, who had been sent to Rome to find lodgings with a view to opening a house there, and who now covered the length and breadth of Italy helping to spread the word about the publications of Alba and Fr Alberione's Society.

Giaccardo settled the boys on the Via Ostiense, about half a mile from St Paul's Basilica, while Maestra Amalia gathered the Daughters just round the corner in Via di Porto Fluviale. They were still a long way from having a place they could call their own; the establishment of a Pauline house in Rome was a distant dream. Their present predicament was more like that of refugees or victims of an earthquake.

By the will and wish of Pius XI

They lived as intruders – almost outlaws. In the first place, the Society of St Paul had no canonical existence, not being officially recognised even by the Bishop of Alba. Secondly, priests and religious from outside Rome need the permission of the Cardinal Vicar to take up residence in the city even on a temporary basis and this could not be granted to an irregular community.

Fr Giaccardo had been granted leave of absence by the Bishop of Alba and had been authorised to say Mass in Rome when he presented his documents to the Vicariate. But this only covered him as an unaccompanied priest, not the young male and female religious, with their printing machinery, their rudimentary school equipment and all the rest of their paraphernalia. Giaccardo eventually took refuge in a pretext suggested to him by the Founder: the establishment would simply be a forwarding address set up in Rome to facilitate the re-distribution of material printed at Alba.

But Giuseppe Giaccardo had too honest a face; he was

no match for the worldly wisdom of Mgr Pascucci of the Roman Vicariate, who by March was writing letters of enquiry to the Bishop of Alba. What was this story about a forwarding address? Where was Fr Giaccardo's material support coming from? What were his real plans? Who were the young men and women he had with him? Did the bishop not know that all of them were in breach of Canon 495 and a cause of serious displeasure to the Cardinal Vicar of Rome?

In due course Mgr Pascucci was to become a friend and admirer of Fr Giaccardo once he had seen with his own eyes what they were really trying to do. And the penniless community of enthusiasts also won the heart of Fr Rosa of the Jesuits, editor of *Civiltà Cattolica*, who later spoke warmly about them to the Pope himself. This opened the way for the position of the Pious Society of St Paul to be regularised through its establishment as an institute of diocesan right by the Bishop of Alba under the authority of Rome. That was just the first step. In the fullness of time Rome would confer further degrees of recognition until the Society became a fully approved institution in the Church.

But Fr Alberione wanted to hurry the process forward. He hoped to omit the formality of diocesan approval and to obtain from the Congregation of Religious an immediate *decretum laudis*, the formal act of welcome of a diocesan institute into the wider Church. In his view the services and achievements recorded over the last few years by his community, with its 425 male members and its 166 women, including the Pious Disciples, merited special consideration.

But Pius XI was a strict canon lawyer; he would not allow the diocesan stage to be omitted. He also made it known that it would be a waste of time trying to present the Society as a single organisation with male and female branches. From that point onwards the application for recognition was concerned only with the male religious family of the Pious Society. Other uncertainties and objections soon began to surface in Rome. Why have a congregation devoted exclusively to the press? Instead of a congregation, could it not be organised as a simple confraternity, a format which would commit the Holy See as little as possible, something a little less out of the ordinary?

The apostle eventually got the better of the jurist in the heart of Pius XI. He had always wanted his pontificate to be one of "re-conquest" and in his first encyclical *Ubi arcano Dei* of 1922 he had urged that the active, missionary and apostolic character of the Church should be given new weight, emphasising the special role of the press in this task. It had been his chosen theme for the celebration of Holy Year in 1925; he had also instituted the liturgical feast of Christ the King, commemorated the Council of Nicea, and promoted the World Missionary Exhibition.

Whilst others discussed whether the Alba community should be considered "a simple association of pious religious and lay persons" the Pope was coming to his own decision, opting for the more daring and novel solution. In James Alberione and his work he recognised a sign of the times. And so on 13 July 1926, having listened once more to Cardinal Laurenti's summary of the whole question, Pius XI gave this clear and unhesitating reply: "Your Eminence, *it is our wish and will* that there should be a religious congregation devoted to 'the good press'."

These words put an end to all speculations about pious associations and other fanciful substitutes. This was an instruction. By express wish of the Pope, the Society of St Paul was to become an authentic religious congregation with public vows, dedicated to the mission of the printed word. On 12 March 1927, the Bishop of Alba signed the diocesan decree granting initial recognition; so in law and in fact the men of the Pauline family officially ceased to be wanderers, a household with neither homeland nor ancestry.

However this recognition applied only to the male community; the women had to begin all over again with a completely separate procedure. The Daughters and the Pious Disciples would need first to obtain authorisation from Rome before applying for diocesan recognition. Fr Alberione set this process in motion on 25 October 1927.

But the Founder had to give up one of his cherished ideas before the application could complete even this first step. He had wanted the Daughters of St Paul to be dressed like other women of the day, without any special habit. He reluctantly accepted that this would not be allowed.

To Rome as mother and teacher

In the letters requesting diocesan approval by the Founder and Fr Giaccardo, the signature of Maestra Thecla never once appears. Her responsibilities were confined to the internal affairs of the Institute. She must often have felt a pang of sympathy when she thought of the Daughters in Rome, so young and facing such difficulties. In fact in November 1926, only a few months after settling into their lodgings, they had received notice to quit and had been compelled to leave the small apartment near the Porto Fluviale. They then found accommodation near to the men in makeshift quarters which lacked many necessities.

Thecla well knew what distance, poverty and insecurity meant: she had experienced it every day at Susa. Many times she had felt a strong wish to go to see her Daughters in Rome, but so far the only one to visit the city had been Fr Alberione. In May 1927 he must have had some inkling of that secret desire because one day he suddenly suggested that she should go with him. He returned after one week; she remained for one more, and the Daughters received "from her heart as mother and teacher" goodness, wisdom and the strength to persevere on the road ahead. After her visit the house was united in heart and soul.

The purpose of Maestra Thecla's journey to Rome was to visit a community of which she was superior. But she also fell victim to the charm of the Eternal City, which she was seeing for the first time. In her personal notes she gives particular emphasis to the spiritual aspect: "To Rome in pilgrimage. Rediscover the spirit of St Peter, St Paul, of the Pope, and return greatly inspired." This new fervour instilled in her heart an intense love for the Apostle, which shone through in all her later teaching. Her notes also record the retreat preached by the Founder, who in that month of May suggested a detailed programme of dedication: "Turn to Mary and allow your spiritual self to be formed by her. As she herself formed Jesus, so she will help to form us."

Fr Alberione returned to Rome in the summer of 1927 and entered into an agreement with the Benedictines to buy St Paul's Vineyard, a property in Via Grottaperfetta, about half a mile from the Basilica of St Paul Outside the Walls. It consisted of a farm house and stabling, and included a generous stretch of uncultivated land with two long rows of vines. Its few rooms, which at that stage were almost uninhabitable, were soon adapted and equipped as kitchen, study place and living accommodation for the Daughters. This purchase gave immense joy to everyone.

It was now November. The draughty hay-loft was transformed into a dormitory as the cold of winter advanced: it even snowed that year. This truly was Bethlehem, and Thecla had her first taste of its poverty in the first week of December. Her reflections on the second Roman retreat were devoted to the examination of her thoughts to see how far they departed from the Gospel: "Jesus says, 'Blessed are the poor', whilst we bless the rich; 'Blessed are the meek', yet we reward those who seek their own advantage at the expense of their neighbour." The desperate situation of the community did not dismay her: it gave them an opportunity to live the Gospel.

The whole Pauline community faced a serious problem in finding ways of distributing its books and periodicals, which by now were coming off the presses in considerable quantities. Clearly it was not enough just to print them. But to spend money on publicity was impossible, and the message would probably not have reached the intended purchasers. So the tasks of circulation and distribution, usually and very properly referred to as "the apostolate", became the first responsibility and particular specialisation of the Daughters of St Paul.

All this called for a different kind of organisation, new methods of work and, last but not least, new clothing. At that time a woman wearing the religious habit hardly needed to introduce herself. Whoever she spoke to – whether it was a bishop, a parish priest or a family on the doorstep – knew immediately who it was they were dealing with. To the nun herself it provided a form of defence; to the person she approached the habit offered a certain guarantee. It also corresponded with the wishes of the Holy See. So in the summer of 1928, at a word from Fr Alberione, Thecla found herself once again a seamstress, or rather a designer, with the task of creating a habit that would distinguish the Daughters of St Paul from other nuns, combining sober appearance, informality, respectability and freedom of movement. In the evenings, rather like conspirators, she and a few other sisters discussed and tried out a variety of ideas. In the end they opted for a long black habit with a jacket and veil of the same colour, the whole effect being strikingly relieved by a stiff collar of pure white.

The Daughters put on the habit together for the first time at a special ceremony on the last Sunday in October 1928, the feast of Christ the King. The scene was worthy of the event. It took place in the great church dedicated to St Paul at Alba, the heart of the Pauline world, a building considerably more imposing than Fr Alberione's other achievements as they stood at that time. But the Founder had determined the scale of the building with the future in mind. This building was not intended as a commemoration of anything in the past; rather, it looked forward with confidence to the future. There, in that vast sacred space, still largely unadorned, the sisters who had contributed in so many ways in its construction donned the religious habit for the first time.

The diocesan decree

Meanwhile the Roman Congregation's dossier on the Daughters of St Paul was becoming more voluminous. They had received indirect support from Pope Pius XI because of his keen interest in the male branch and later, following his wish, the Congregation of Religious left the decision entirely to him. The Pontiff insisted not only on a careful examination of the documentation, but also of the situation on the ground, calling for inspections to be carried out on the premises to ensure that everything was in order. Then when everything had been examined and checked he gave his consent in December 1928. The way ahead was now clear, and on 15 March 1929 Bishop Re of Alba signed the Latin decree which established the Pious Society of the Daughters of St Paul as a religious congregation of diocesan right. He confirmed Thecla as head of the Institute, referring to her by her baptismal name: *"Eligimus Sororem Merlo Theresam..."*

These words were no more than a recognition of the existing situation. Four days later the process was completed by the act of public and perpetual profession performed by the Prima Maestra and her four Councillors: Eufrosina Binello (Maestra Margherita), Vittoria Perron (Maestra Brigida), Angela Raballo (Maestra Teresa) and Maria Soldano (Maestra Edvige).

The Pious Disciples were also included in the new female community; the Roman Congregation would not agree to Fr Alberione's original arrangements for a separate entity. Thus Maestra Thecla found herself at the head of a more complex organisation, in which overall unity had to take precedence over the specialised tasks of its two component parts. When in 1947 the Pious Disciples finally became a religious congregation in their own right, the first to accept the new situation was Thecla herself.

In one of her earliest conferences given to the Daughters she spoke at length on the subject of obedience. As always she used plain language and simple expressions, avoiding solemn quotations. Here are her own words as they were committed to writing at the time by one of the Daughters: "We have been told that this is to be the year of obedience. The virtue of obedience is indispensable to the religious life, because if we do not obey we are not good religious. Our obedience must not be proportionate to a person's rank – full obedience to one: not quite so full to another. We must see Our Lord in the person who gives the order even though the one commanding may be a younger colleague. In obeying her we do the Lord's will.

"Similarly, we must not make distinctions between one task and another, but allow ourselves to be freely used. Only in this way can we say we are fully co-operating in our vocation. We must deny our own will in order to do the will of God as it is expressed by our superiors when they give us instructions, without pausing to think who they may be."

The whole Bible for everyone

Thecla and the Daughters had not simply been waiting for canonical recognition before embracing the Founder's new ideas. They belonged to an enterprise which did not measure success according to modern business criteria, though it taught a lesson to the entire Church of its time. Sister Natalina Spada, a Daughter of St Paul, an eye-witness and a fellow-worker, gives an insight into the attitudes of Alberione and the whole Pauline family: "Another of Fr Alberione's ventures – largely forgotten now because it failed to achieve the results he hoped for – remains a monument to the prophetic vision of Founder. This was the printing of the Bible in six languages and 18 editions. To carry through this project Fr Alberione had to be quite sure that the Daughters themselves knew what the Bible was…"

And by that he meant the whole Bible, the Old Testament and the New, from Genesis to the Apocalypse, something unheard of in those times. The very word "bible" itself was used with circumspection, and there was little danger that it would ever fall from the lips of a preacher. Fr Alberione was of a different opinion, "The Bible is a collection of 72 books written under divine inspiration. It is God's letter to men and women."

So it was to men that it had to be delivered, and above all, to Catholic households, where no one, or almost no one, among the faithful was familiar with its message. Even a man like Carlo Carretto, one of the most prolific lay spiritual writers of this century, had to admit: "I made my first discovery of the Bible at the age of about 20, and without doubt it was one of the greatest strokes of good fortune I ever had in my life…" People discovered the Bible either by chance or at the cost of much persistence, having known nothing of it for most of their adolescence, with the exception perhaps of a few passages, a few characters. In other words, most people had read very little of God's letter.

Fr Alberione wanted Catholics to read it all. He accordingly decided to print it, but not before he had made it known to the men and women of his own communities. Once again it is Sister Maria Natalina who tells us how this was organised: "The Theologian began what seemed like an endless series of instructions on the Bible to his young men and women. We began with several periods of general introduction to biblical studies and then one or more lessons on each of the sacred books. These took place every Sunday and the whole programme lasted at least a couple of years."

Thecla was among those who followed this course and she took careful notes on each book like everyone else. She must have been especially struck by the story of Job, to which she gave a particularly full treatment. At the end of the programme after the final entry she expresses her happiness for this extraordinary enrichment of the soul. However her emotions, even in these personal papers, are expressed with her usual sobriety – a simple repetition of the words: "Thanks be to God!"

The Daughters who worked on the production of the Bible had to endure hard work and long hours. Thecla feared that some of them might even become ill and she went to Fr Alberione to confide these fears. Their exchange was a short one, as was the reply she carried straight back to the Daughters: "He has assured me that you will be perfectly well until the work is finished."

And finish it they did. The Christmas of 1931 was a very special one because it was also the celebration of the completion of the enormous task. To mark the event they placed, alongside the traditional figures in the crib, a large basket piled high with bibles printed in different languages for the readers of the whole world.

Meanwhile the moment had arrived to set up a permanent and properly organised system for the sale of books and newspapers. The Daughters were and would remain writers, printers, and publishers, but their principal role in the international front line would always be in distribution and sales. There was no shortage of ideas about how to improve the performance of their task.

At a meeting of the Council in May 1927, Thecla spoke of buying a vehicle and mentioned the names of two sisters who might learn to drive it. At that time the very thought of a nun at the wheel of a car would have been dismissed by many people as mad, but the Prima Maestra got her way in due course, taking one cautious step at a time.

Their first experience for developing an effective distribution technique was gained at Alba and in the surrounding district, where they worked out what would later become one of their standard methods. The beatification of Don Bosco was due to take place on 2 June 1929, an important religious event and a particular cause for local celebration. Exploiting the topicality of the occasion, they printed a popular version of the life of the future Blessed, which was very well received. So Don Bosco – himself a writer, publisher and pioneer of the Catholic press – opened many doors in the diocese of Alba to the Society and the Daughters, who were able to offer people the Bible, the Gospels, lives of St Teresa of Lisieux and of the future saint, Gemma Galgani, as well as a suitable selection of adventure stories.

The experiment was extended to the other dioceses of Piedmont and to other regions including Rome, where the sisters from Via Grottaperfetta covered both the city and the surrounding countryside.

Maria Natalina Spada recalls how they organised local door-to-door sales: "We left for the villages around Alba and Asti, each of us carrying two or three packets of books. We always travelled in twos, usually a sister accompanied by a postulant or a student. We reached the chosen village by horse and cart or in the Fiat, which Fr Manera would drive. We looked for hospitality with the local nuns or with the parish priest and from time to time we would stay with a family. The Theologian taught us in his meditations always to conduct ourselves with humility and faith: in faith because we were offering people the Gospel and the lives of the saints; in humility because as individuals we were full of deficiencies and perhaps also of sin. We were to stay together at all times, to be watchful, and to help each other in need. One would offer the book whilst the other prayed. If the book was refused we at least left a leaflet, but always in humility. Mother Thecla often used this method of presentation herself, working with one or other of her sisters, and then offering advice which was always constructive and practical."

Thecla's way was to involve herself personally in the apostolate. It could hardly have been otherwise, for everything the Daughters were attempting was as new for her as it was for them. She had to attend to everything during this period of trial and error: how to greet people, how to deal with both friendly and hostile receptions on the doorstep, how to introduce the reason for their visit, the words used in the presentation, and the inevitable questions about prices and payment.

All this was completely new experience for them all.

Previously they had prayed and worked at home. It was a hard life, but they were protected and reassured by the walls that surrounded them and by the rhythm of routines which had become second nature. They had also enjoyed the feeling of living as part of a group with superiors close at hand. It was another matter entirely to go from door to door, not knowing what to expect next, needing to take many small decisions on the spur of the moment and to manage everything by themselves. This was why Thecla needed to accompany her Daughters, to be part of her team as they explored paths where the Church had never set foot before. She had to work out rules of conduct on which no Council, no Synod or Chapter had ever pronounced. These experiences with her own sisters were a vital part of her formation as Prima Maestra. It was the only way she could learn.

By observing each other at work, seeing how some approaches produced better results than others, the professed Daughters soon learned how to train those with less experience. The task confirmed Thecla in her native virtue of simplicity. It was a virtue now further refined by her progress in the spiritual life, one which she realised was indispensable for the Congregation as a whole if it was to be an effective bearer of the Gospel message. "Simplicity is a characteristic of our Institute: we must guard and protect it, resisting and doing our best to eliminate everything that tends to make us pompous and petty." For Thecla, simplicity consisted of "that natural grace, that special combination of exterior qualities which befit a nun, qualities which, if you do not have them at the age of 20, you are unlikely to acquire even by the time you're 30."

This was her purpose: to reach the hearts of her girls as quickly as possible. She paid particular attention to the youngest ones, deeply conscious that it was in those first years that the seeds of success or failure were sown.

Here too Thecla was unable to look back to any authoritative tradition or famous teachers who might help her to put Alberione's general ideas into practice. In the personal counselling of her sisters she had only her own spiritual resources to draw on, together of course with those few but essential notions which she had picked up within her own family and perfected in the light of their example. Those were the marks of character for which her father Ettore Merlo was consulted with such confidence at Castagnito – his honest personal style and way of life, the straightforwardness of his words and actions. Whether in smiling or solemn mood, Thecla was always completely straightforward. If she noticed that some girl seemed to stand in awe of her she would find an early opportunity to take her on one side and reassure her in the most kindly way.

The Prima Maestra had now personally supervised the spiritual formation of her sisters and shared most of their experiences of the mission. Fr Alberione now wanted her to lead another new venture: the Daughters of St Paul were to open book centres in various Italian cities. The storms of protest aroused by this initiative were foreseeable : "A shop run by religious! Nuns in the retail trade! Where on earth will all this end?"

Thecla was completely unmoved. The Daughters went ahead and succeeded in opening their centres with all the necessary permits from the town hall and the prefect's office, their licence paid for and displayed as the law required. The next stage was the growth around these book centres of small communities of Daughters, who continued to carry out all their duties and observances as religious whilst running a sales outlet.

In those days the house in Rome was regarded as an extension of the Mother house at Alba, and so when the first book centre was opened at Salerno, south of Naples, Fr Alberione celebrated the departure of those chosen for this mission with the solemnity which he typically reserved for great occasions. In "The story of the houses", the archive of the Congregation we read: "On 1 November 1928, three days after the clothing of the Daughters, between Vespers and supper, the Primo Maestro called the community back into church and exposed the Blessed Sacrament. He handed a copy of the Gospel to the five sisters who were about to leave and preached a beautiful homily. The ceremony ended with solemn Benediction. That function marked the opening of the first of the branch houses."

Enthusiasm and misunderstandings

To establish themselves in a new city meant, first of all, finding temporary lodgings, then obtaining suitable premises for the book centre, opening it for business as soon as possible and bringing it to people's attention. It was also essential to make early contact with the local bishop, the clergy, the parishes and lay associations to explain that there was no great commercial organisation behind the centre, just a tiny religious community with its own local superior. They worked to make themselves known in the surrounding districts, the smaller towns, villages and hamlets. Little versed in the world of trains and buses, the sisters, carrying suit-cases full of books, covered a formidable number of miles on foot. They often took wrong turnings and missed short cuts; but they thought nothing of distances, even though this often meant they were not able to get back to town by the evening.

In some cases the young women would spend the whole week moving from one village to the next. They had mixed experiences, most of them warm and happy, though on some occasions the welcome was less than cordial. Sometimes they would have to spend the night under the spreading canopies of a vineyard; sometimes they found themselves observing involuntary fasts, not daring to buy food in the shops and even less to set foot in the taverns.

A few parish priests distrusted them, unable to credit that these women with their cases of books were genuine Catholic nuns. More rarely they encountered blank rejection, hostility and even suspicious glances from the police.

A few of the Daughters were discouraged by these experiences, though they persevered obediently. For others this was a wonderful challenge, from which they returned tired but always happy.

Maestra Thecla, following their adventures at first in person and later by letter, realised that their lives as religious must continue to be rooted in the basic principles of the Congregation. But it was equally clear that customs, timetables and the domestic rules of Alba could not simply be transferred into the regimes of the branch houses. She therefore began a careful revision of the regulations, adapting them to the very different circumstances of work in the field. For example, she laid down that local superiors should allow a weekly rest period for Daughters returning from long journeys. She also told them to encourage the young women to talk freely about their difficulties and to listen to them with attention and respect so that lessons might be learned from their complaints.

She began a series of circular letters. These documents are still of great interest today for their notes and comments on the spiritual life. These notes are invariably down-to-earth and indeed are often found casually interpolated among purely administrative instructions.

The first of them is dated 29 December 1929, and Thecla devotes most of her affectionate concern to the sisters' problems in settling into their new role. She begins by inviting them to model themselves on Our Lady: "Taking Mary as our leader and guide, let us meditate on her virtues: her modesty, her prudence in speech, her constant contemplation of Jesus' words, which she kept stored in her heart; her charity towards all – whether close neighbours or people bringing work to Joseph – her overriding kindness, which embraced everyone whilst avoiding familiarity with anyone. Is that a Model that appeals to you?"

We seem almost to hear a whisper of nostalgia for the years at Susa. There it had been easy for them to know what to do in new or difficult situations; there they always received courtesy in return. Now the Daughters were exposed to the possibility of unpleasantness and even to the risk of danger. "You are like doves alighting on mud. Remember, though, that Our Lady had to go through worse experiences, where the mud came up to her eyes; but, like the spotless dove that she is, she never once soiled her feet."

Naturally enough they were more successful in some things than others, and from time to time they had to pay heavily for their inexperience. There were problems within the Congregation, and they had to face up to occasional individual inadequacies. But somehow they picked themselves up and went forward again, achieving results which today seem truly astonishing. Their survival and success is partly explained by the less sophisticated times they lived in, but much of their achievement was undoubtedly due to their own interior strength.

Those first Daughters came from families and from a generation well acquainted with the rough edges of life, with heavy work meanly rewarded and with sacrifice. Having been brought up in times when hardship was the common lot, they were well equipped to face challenges and overcome obstacles.

As their book centres became better established they began to involve themselves in the religious life of the towns where they worked. Among their initiatives were the Gospel Days, a parish-based celebration of the Word of God devised by Fr Alberione. They were seen as a daring innovation at the time, but they proved popular with laity and clergy alike. By promoting new ideas like this the Daughters gradually transformed what began as an ordinary retail outlet into a meeting place, somewhere to find new friends, new supporters, and – most important of all – new vocations to the Society of St Paul.

Maestra Thecla was most insistent about the vocations. Indeed she was insistent about most things: from the daily prayer observances to the annual stock-taking reports, which had to arrive at Alba not later than 6 January each year. "And please also make sure that your monthly accounts aren't late; we need to check everything here as soon as possible."

The great crash of 1929 was first felt in America but its effects eventually reached Italy and life became much harder. Large numbers of industrial workers were laid off, trade was at a standstill and towards the end of 1930 the government took the unprecedented step of imposing a wage reduction of eight percent. State employees had their salaries cut by 10%. Government pressure was brought to bear to reduce rents and the cost of food, and some people may have believed Augusto Turati, secretary of the Fascist Party, when he said that the 1,000 Lire note would become so rare that it would be worth framing.

The sisters working at the book centres were severely affected by this situation and the resulting unemployment. Cheques were dishonoured; neighbouring shops went into liquidation. There was hunger in many families, and debts with shopkeepers mounted. The economic forecasts in every newspaper were of continuing recession throughout the world and no one dared guess how long the bad news would continue.

Thecla had an answer to the crash which was all her own. She wrote to the Daughters urging them to press on with their efforts on behalf of the Bible: "Everyone is complaining about the economic crisis, but don't let that frighten you. The Church achieved its greatest results during the most horrific times. Provided we do not offend him by sin we have the Almighty on our side." Nevertheless the sale of books was becoming much more difficult. In one diocese the bishop warned the Daughters not to be surprised if people refused to buy. At the same time he did not want to discourage them: "Don't show yourselves too disappointed. If you can't leave a good book you can at least leave a good word, something to cheer people up, a smile."

Those were words of advice from a wise pastor. They evidently appealed to Thecla because she reproduced them in a circular to all the Daughters, adding a few comments of her own to temper the eagerness of any sister who might be a little too keen on making a sale. Sometimes, she said, "we forget that the first form of persuasion is good example. Why do we publicise our books? To offer help to people. Well then, why should we use unkind words when we meet a cool reception, or even when people greet us with insults? That is just the moment when we should be practising humility and gentleness. Do we want to be true disciples of Jesus? Well then, let us imitate Him! Let's remember that humble and gentle words spoken in reply to discourtesy and refusal are seeds that will eventually germinate and produce great good."

Here we have the essence of Thecla. The kindly and ever-faithful upholder of the principles of the Primo Maestro knows just what to say and how to say it. The note of encouragement is truly hers, especially the repeated reminder of the need for humility. Thecla might justly be called Sister *Magnificat*, for she always harks back in her words and actions to Mary's canticle. This letter makes a precise reference to it – at the place where God, the Father and Creator, appears almost to show a human preference for one virtue of his servant above all her others: "for he has regarded the low estate of his handmaiden" (Luke 1:48).

Spurred on by the Maestra's humility and courage, Thecla's sisters were gradually becoming familiar figures in many parts of Italy. They were discussed in bishops' palaces and in thousands of parish halls. Though still few in number, their voice resounded throughout the land. Their achievements enabled Fr Alberione to send glowing reports to the Congregation of Religious in Rome.

If anyone had dared object in the summer of 1931 to the "outlandish" idea of an order of nuns dedicated to the printed word, Alberione would have been able to reply with some impressive facts. The Daughters of St Paul had visited 246 dioceses in Italy; thanks to their efforts, no less than 3,000 parish libraries had been started; subscribers to the religious periodicals of the Society had reached 1,300,000. All this had been due largely to the efforts of the sisters. In addition, 50,000 Bibles had been distributed, whilst altogether a million copies of the Gospels, the letters of St Paul and a life of Jesus had been placed in the hands of readers throughout Italy. In short, as Fr Alberione proudly told the Roman authorities, "The Daughters of St Paul are spreading the teaching of the Church through the medium of the printed word." It had once been a mere hope and, according to many, a vain illusion. Now it was a fact.

To the Americas to sow the seed of the Word

In 1931 Fr Alberione was 47 and he still spent at least four hours of every day on his knees – a professional penitent, one might almost say, living more in the next world than in this. He seemed to walk in fear that the world might end at any moment: like Gregory the Great, who had been taken from his monastery to be made Pope, and who led endless processions around the city of Rome chanting the *Miserere*. Yet after the torments of the plague, after the Lombards had ravaged Italy and the Imperial government had fled from Rome, it was the same Gregory who revealed himself, for all his failing health, as a prodigy of energy, renewing every aspect of life – civil, religious, economic and military. In the world of the Pauline community something of the same kind seems to have happened to the fragile and unpredictable Theologian, James Alberione.

"He was capable", according to Silvano Gratilli, "of keeping us in church for hours, meditating on the Four Last Things, examining our consciences on the denial of the senses and the cultivation of the virtues. It was not much different from one of the stricter monastic regimes. Then the next minute he would be ordering us to go out into the highways and byways of the world to publicise 'the good press', leaping onto our bicycles and driving off in cars, to the considerable scandal of right-thinking people – not to mention bigots and puritans."

Death, Judgement, Hell and Heaven – the Four Last Things: the Primo Maestro insisted in his frail voice they had to be meditated on every day. Then without changing his tone he would announce that he was sending someone to America. He already knew who was to go and when they would leave. He had also decided on the financial arrangements for the enterprise: no contribution whatever from the Society of St Paul. These new apostles would have to raise their own expenses from well-wishers and relations. Foolhardy, tyrannical and absurd as it may seem, this was literally how he did it. There was absolutely no overall plan. Some time before this he had written to his communities: "We are ready to take on the world; it would be a tragedy if we did not grasp the opportunity." At the time these words seemed like ambitious hopes, distant objectives in the long perspective of history; but James Alberione was in fact thinking of the near future. One day, after one of his regular meditations on the Four Last Things, he drew aside two of his priests and told them quite simply that they were to go to South America. And he meant straight away.

In 1931 there was still a great deal to be done within the Pauline family in and indeed at Alba itself. But then there was even more for the Apostle Paul to do in Asia Minor when the man appeared to him in a dream "standing beseeching him and saying, 'Come over to Macedonia and help us'." So it was with Alberione, who had decided that the moment had arrived to set out for the New World; and immediately, as in the Acts of the Apostles.

On 6 August 1931 Fr Sebastiano Trosso and Fr Benedetto Boano boarded the Italian liner *Conte Verde* at Genoa. Two weeks later they disembarked at the Brazilian port of Santos; Boano travelled inland to establish himself at São Paulo whilst Trosso sailed on to Buenos Aires in Argentina.

The money for this first journey was obtained in a way which was to become typical. Unable to obtain a single lira from the Founder, Fr Boano thought of approaching a man from Verona who had been helpful to him in the past, a lawyer by the name of Martini. But this involved going to Verona in person, which in turn meant finding the fare for the train.

At that point Boano thought of Thecla, and she was somehow able to produce 900 Lire, considerably more than the cost of the return fare. As a result of this journey he obtained 10,000 Lire from his benefactor, equivalent to a bank clerk's salary for a year and quite enough to pay the ocean passages of both priests. They even had 3,000 Lire left after they arrived in Brazil, but on hearing of this the Primo Maestro wrote asking for the surplus to be sent back to him.

The surplus was no doubt spent on others who were soon to be sent as reinforcements. Meanwhile Alberione was already thinking about the USA, and in particular of New York. He waited until the spiritual exercises were completed and then made a similar proposal to Fr Francis Borrano. He would have to find the money for the journey himself "and also enough in addition to be able to start working". Fr Borrano embarked on the *Roma* and arrived in New York in early October 1931.

What was expected of members of the Congregation who were sent overseas is explained in a letter from Fr Alberione to these first pioneers and then circulated among the whole community. Their job was to "spread the divine Word by means of the press. Present it with the same warmth of heart as Jesus the Master did when He preached, with the passion of St Paul, with the grace and humility which Our Lady showed when she consented to became the Mother of the Incarnate Word."

His directions on editorial policy were precise: pastoral values before everything. "Your publications must serve a pastoral purpose, the kind of thing that St Paul would have written if he had lived today. Your spiritual and material methods must also reflect pastoral values; likewise your methods of distribution. That is what you are being sent to do." He promised to send reinforcements "as soon as you send back the wherewithal," and he also gave this instruction: "First you should ensure that the men's house is well established; later you will need to set up a house for the women, which should be at least five minutes' walk away." The jobs of printing, sales and administration were to be kept separate. "Your apostolic missions should be united only in the sense that you operate in parallel."

So women too would leave for distant shores. Fr Alberione had used the word "later", but in his vocabulary that usually meant with as little delay as possible. Thecla was aware of all this, not only in a general way like everyone else, but in increasing detail as the date for their departure came closer.

An undated note, probably from 1931, has come to light in one of the Pauline houses in which Fr Alberione says: "Prima Maestra, it is an *excellent* idea to send a *good* number of Daughters of St Paul overseas... Japan, India, Brazil, Ireland, China, Spain, Portugal, the United States, France etc are all waiting to hear God's Word from you."

For some time she had been preparing the first candidates for their journeys, with India and Japan particularly in mind. She was also making careful plans on the material front so that the Daughters could leave with their passage money and enough to keep them whilst they were settling in. It was her responsibility to look after all this side of the venture and she was never found wanting in her plans or her timing.

But above all she prepared them spiritually, for she wanted them to be fully aware that the essential nature of their work was missionary. She would never tire of repeating it even in later years: "My good Sisters, though we're now well established in Italy we must develop our apostolate abroad. Our Lord has given us a much wider field, the Missions. And don't let us talk about overseas houses; we should always speak of the Missions." She methodically instilled into each one of them the quality that she herself had learned with such joy from the Primo Maestro – a serene and total confidence in God, and not just to buoy up their optimism, but to stimulate their fighting spirit and power of endurance in all situations.

Here in her own words is her recollection of the women's Congregation in those early days: "At times we were so discouraged that we hardly knew which way to turn. But for my part I was never afraid – despite all the gossip about us outside and the crosses we had to bear within the house. We had the greatest faith in the Theologian... and our hearts were at peace in the knowledge that we were in the hands of a father who wanted nothing but our good. He once said to me, 'I sometimes think that you place too much trust in the Theologian; you should only trust in God.' This made me think very hard and I said to myself, 'Certainly, I do have great faith in Our Lord, but I also trust the Theologian because I know that he is sent by God. Wherever he goes, I can be sure that I will make no mistake if I follow.'"

There was a need for the highest commitment in the Daughters who were to go overseas. Maestra Thecla used to slip a letter of encouragement into their luggage, a tactful farewell present which would give them strength during the journey and in their early difficulties. These letters, always so full of affectionate inspiration, became one of her traditions. Here is one example. "Before you leave our dear but provisional homeland I send you a greeting and a wish that comes from the bottom of my heart... a wish that you should see this new country where you are going to live as an opportunity to work for your own holiness. Do try to make yourselves truly holy... Don't be discouraged if you cannot see the good you are doing. Most of the good we do for people is achieved when we ourselves are hidden. Our unseen sacrifices count for more than an apostolate that draws attention to itself... You leave in the name of the Most Holy Trinity, as we shall all leave this world for eternity in that same holy name. May the triune God – the heavenly Father who made you, his divine Son who died for you, and the Holy Spirit who sanctified you–bless you abundantly! Begin your apostolate on the ship by giving a good example of earnestness and true religious spirit."

One of the first sisters to leave for an oversees mission was Maestra Addolorata Baldi. At 21 years of age she was leader of a party consisting of just herself and Margherita Metilde Gerlotto, one of the first Pious Disciples. They were told to go to Brazil. They left Genoa on 6 October 1931 on the *Conte Rosso* with two unordained clerics in theology and a lay brother. These last were already expected as reinforcements and Fr Boano was waiting to greet them on the quayside at Santos. But he knew absolutely nothing about the sisters and he was thunderstruck when he saw them: "I wrote to the Primo Maestro telling him not to send you!" he exclaimed.

There was nothing to be done about it now; there they were. To make matters worse the local archbishop did not want them. They found a first refuge at São Paulo with the Missionaries of the Sacred Heart, the Cabrini Sisters, who worked among the Italian immigrant population. They had to put aside the religious habit. Addolorata and Margherita went into hiding to pray and to study Portuguese. After a couple of months they found that Thecla had been right. The good Lord had heard their plea: the archbishop had changed his mind, given his blessing, and asked them to dress as nuns again. So they were able to set about their work, finding a place to live, starting up a book centre and bringing other young women over from Italy to begin their rounds. At last they were missionaries! There was a repetition of the same scene at Buenos Aires, where the *Conte Verde* docked on 31 December 1931. Here Fr Trosso was waiting to greet Fr Giuseppe Fossati and was astonished to see two sisters of St Paul, Caterina Carbone and Ester Innocenti, coming down the gangway. He too had been told absolutely nothing about their arrival.

It was the same story all over again: improvised accommodation arranged by Fr Trosso, the search for a base in Buenos Aires, and at last a start on the job of making themselves known. Here at least they had the consolation of a friendly welcome from the local clergy, but difficulties of another kind hindered their first steps in the apostolate. The world crisis struck the Argentine economy with particular force, based as it mainly was on massive exports of meat, which fell disastrously, and on British credits, which dried up. The government of President Irigoyen fell in 1930, to be replaced by a military dictatorship under General Uriburu. But the crisis continued unabated. Uriburu was in turn deposed in February 1932, and after regular elections Augustin Pedro Justo took over as President. His programme imposed the most stringent economies on the whole country.

In short, it was a bad time to be committing money to a new venture. Nevertheless this is just what the sisters did, mindful of Maestra Thecla and of her very personal ideas on how to deal with emergencies. In the end everything turned out for the best; by 1933 they had got together the essentials of a printing operation – a platen press, a stitching machine and a guillotine. It was enough to make a start.

We have already heard about the arrival of the first Daughters in the United States. This time the sisters, Maestra Paula Cordero and a companion, were fully expected. The enterprising Fr Borrano was at the quayside to meet them on 28 June 1932 and as usual they found their first welcome in a friendly convent. They stayed with the Sisters of St John the Baptist and then found lodgings in the Bronx. Here too the archbishop, Cardinal Hayes, was unenthusiastic about their mission and the two sisters, with others who arrived later, devoted their early efforts exclusively to the Italian community, enjoying no more than tolerance from the local church authorities. Indeed there were those who urged them to leave New York, pointedly inviting them to "try some other diocese".

But they were not to be discouraged. Thecla had taught them to hold firm, and they simply replied that if the Primo Maestro and the Prima Maestra had sent them there it was God's will that they should stay. They did stay, unruffled during their long wait for acceptance, until the archbishop, or one of his frowning subordinates, was converted. "Now that they're here," observed the cardinal, "they may as well remain."

Thecla kept in touch with developments in America and wrote weekly letters from Alba. The establishment of printing and distribution operations and book centres overseas brought new problems. It was easier to make wrong decisions. For example, in order to minimise occupancy taxes it was not appropriate in the early days to have the centre in too prominent a position. Large signs were to be avoided; a simple picture of St Paul was all that was needed to show people who they were. She also emphasised the distinction clearly drawn by Fr Alberione between the tasks of the male Congregation and those of the Daughters. Besides keeping their establishments physically separate it was essential that they also kept to their separate fields of action. And she never ceased to reassure them: "Do the best you can; take your time and don't worry."

Indeed the Daughters did their level best. But they were not saints, and from time to time Maestra Thecla would hear echoes of unpleasantness, reports about arguments, failures of understanding and mistakes at work. She was naturally very sensitive to situations of this kind and in her replies she took care to encourage rather than rebuke, though she was never unduly indulgent. If she noticed shortcomings she would not hesitate to draw attention to them. If she was grieved by anyone's behaviour she would say so quite frankly, as though she had her sisters around her at Alba. Being across the seas in the front line did not excuse any relaxation of effort along the path to holiness.

In a letter to one of the sisters in Brazil in November 1932 we read: "Write to me often and tell me everything: all the bad things that you've done, that you're sorry for, that you won't do again... And now be at peace! Carry on working as hard as you can to find humility of heart; don't bother too much if people judge you as good or bad. St Paul says: 'It is the Lord who judges me' (1 Cor 4:4). You can tell me anything and everything, just as you see it. I know you well, so I will also know what value to put on things. In fact you don't say anything about what you're doing. And yet I have the right to know. I don't want long newsy letters, but I must have the essentials... You must tell me everything important. When you are more humble, a better sister, Our Lord will bless you with greater insights. Submit willingly, and know how to accept that you may be wrong, even when you are sure you are in the right. If you loved God more you would hardly notice these things."

In certain letters to groups of the sisters she used quite forceful language, as in this one dealing with some failure of charity: "Why do you squabble over a trifle? Why, as soon as one of you wants a thing, does someone else immediately want something different? Why, after so many years in the religious life, do you find it hard to do what ordinary Christians find quite easy? Why do I keep hearing of things that cause me so much anguish? Do you want me to tell you? It's because there is still enormous pride in all of you! Because each of you wants to have her own way! Because you have little love of God! You all send me greetings and good wishes for Easter. If only I could read just this: 'We love each other; we are all of the same heart!' That would be enough. I should be happy. Is it too much to hope for?"

Chapter Four

LIKE A GREAT TREE

Radiating confidence in all directions

From Maestra Thecla Merlo to Fr Alberione: "Reverend Primo Maestro, I am writing to ask you a great kindness – that you will always tell us what you think. If we do something wrong, correct us as a father would his daughters. You know that I am in your hands. Use me as though I were a mere handkerchief. [1] I am constantly afraid that I do not act for the best and that I may lead the Daughters astray. When I find that you have not spoken to me for a while I begin to feel uneasy. I am not sure if this is a good thing, but I want you to know everything. I notice that I am becoming very uncharitable. Pray that God will be merciful to me! God be thanked! Poor Sister Teresa."

From Fr Alberione to Thecla: "Have trust: always and above everything! There are countless reasons for confidence – even more so in the month of May. Rely on providence for spiritual graces, especially for the true love of God. As for the Daughters and the apostolate, trust in God and try always to have the right intentions. With my blessing. M Alberione."

This highly-charged fragment of correspondence is on a single sheet. The Founder has written his reply in the margin of Thecla's own note to save time and paper. In the Pauline family the idea of poverty embraces a strict economy in everything consumed, from scraps of paper to working materials. By express order of Fr Alberione only one thing

---

[1] The symbol of the handkerchief conveyed the idea of being adaptable and flexible – ready to be of service in any way. In the years before the second Vatican Council there was the tradition among the Daughters of receiving a "profession handkerchief" at the end of the noviciate, to be kept as a reminder of this readiness.

was freely available in this young community and that was bread.

Let us return to the brief exchange of messages (to which no precise date can be attributed). There we see Thecla not only very responsive to orders, but almost thirsting for an obedience which will provide security, a kind of guarantee. She openly confesses the need to be directed and supported, her fear of making mistakes, her conviction that she has already made many.

She certainly did make some – precisely because she was not the kind of woman who automatically did as she was told. There were many who at first sight dismissed her as a mere disciplinarian, and her energetic style of giving orders sometimes disconcerted girls when they first arrived in the community. But she was not deceived about her true self: she examined her conscience as though she had to earn the position of Prima Maestra anew each day. It was a title she never used when addressing Fr Alberione; and he too in certain cases, as above, limited himself to a simple initial.

It was certainly no easy task for Thecla to become "Prima Maestra" in the fullest sense, to perform all the duties of the office, to confirm her authority in the developing young household of the Daughters of St Paul. For one thing she and her sisters had chosen to live in that "corrupt and corrupting world" from which others preached the need to escape as the only hope of salvation. Yet they threw themselves into it with all the eagerness of youth, accepting a challenge for which there could be no real preparation and which no one had ever tackled before, not even Fr Alberione himself. Hers was a much harder lot than that of the superiors of monastic communities. They remain in the same place, observe the same rule, encounter the same temptations and the same opportunities for hard-won holiness as their predecessors over the centuries. In a monastery everything has already happened before and to every question there is an answer which has stood the test of time.

Thecla, on the other hand, had to work out new methods of leadership and command for herself, and from time to time she needed the medicine of humility to correct her inborn impetuosity: "Yes, it's true that I'm impulsive. It runs in the family. I am well aware of it and afterwards I am always sorry." Then she would move straight on to something else. Once she had trodden the road of humility she felt free again and full of confidence.

La Famiglia Cristiana *is launched by a small group of women*

Thecla was now ready to bring out a new and somewhat different kind of publication suggested by Fr Alberione. He always insisted that St Paul's press should have no taboos: it ought to be able to deal with all aspects of the human condition: "not just to talk about religion, but to speak in a Christian way about everything."

He now had in mind a publication which would follow that policy to the letter and which would be attractive and useful to family members of all ages. He wanted to create something that would appeal, but on a much vaster scale, to the same readership as the *Gazzetta d'Alba* did in its area.

The year 1931 was hardly the best time to start a new Catholic paper in Italy. Quite apart from the economic crisis, in the wake of the Concordat, there was a bitter running battle between the Fascist régime and Catholic Action, which stood accused of intervening in the political arena instead of confining its efforts to the blameless world of devotion. Many prominent people known to be hostile to fascism had been recruited into its ranks and it was openly competing with the official trade unions. Trivial incidents easily degenerated into brawls: for example Catholic Action cycling clubs might raise the papal flag instead of the tricolour, and a day's sport would end in a fight.

Pius XI was quick to intervene in person, strongly denouncing "the campaign of forcible entries, occupations and confiscations of Catholic Action premises and the assaults against its members... often accompanied by bloody violence, with small defenceless groups of Our sons and daughters finding themselves set upon by the mob." Some Fascist extremists talked about arresting all the bishops; others confined themselves to banning or boycotting processions. Even at Alba there were signs of hostility. But the confrontation eventually came to an end and an agreement was reached which placed Catholic Action under the jurisdiction of diocesan bishops.

Meanwhile, ignoring the storms outside, Fr Alberione's plans went ahead and the first number of *La Famiglia Cristiana* (The Christian Family) duly appeared. It was subtitled "For women and children" and cost 20 cents or 8 Lire for a year's subscription. There were just 12 pages in black and white (16 from February 1932) and the front cover carried a picture of the Nativity. Three Daughters of St Paul shared the functions of editorial, production and distribution: Maestra Nazarena Morando, Maestra Ignazia Balla and Maestra Filippina Badanelli. The managing editor was Maestra Rosa Capra. Other sisters helped out, but the main burden fell on the three permanent staff, each of them writing two or three articles a week under different pseudonyms. July 1932 saw the first front cover to be printed in colour and in the meantime the masthead was changed to indicate a change in editorial policy. The name was changed to *Famiglia Cristiana – settimanale religioso morale* (Christian Family – a weekly magazine about religion and morals) and it was no longer aimed exclusively at women and young girls. It came under the management of Fr Luigi Occelli and other members of the Society of St Paul and eventually went on to deal with the needs and problems of all members of the family.

Fr Alberione used to say that you should always begin in miniature – from Bethlehem – and that was how the Daughters started with the new title. Nevertheless they printed 18,000 copies of the first issue – extremely ambitious for those times – but the sisters worked so effectively on publicity and distribution that the circulation gradually began to rise. Fr Luigi Zanoni took over as managing editor in 1938 and eventually the Daughters concerned themselves chiefly with promoting the title.

And so it was at Alba in 1931 that the Daughters of St Paul launched *Famiglia Cristiana*, the publication which in the course of time would become the most successful Catholic weekly magazine in the world.

In 1929 the Society of St Paul decided to establish its own paper mill, for which Fr Alberione bought machinery costing one and a half million Lire; in the economic conditions of the time such an investment seemed to be beyond all reason. Nor did he stop at that. In 1932 he ordered from Germany the most modern rotary press on the market to provide capacity to print Pauline periodicals which had still to be developed and launched – this whilst everyone else was selling assets to convert into bullion or husbanding their reserves in other ways.

It is unlikely that Alberione would ever have noticed the singular parallel between his own actions and those of the new Democratic President of the United States, Franklin Delano Roosevelt, who was elected in 1932. Here was a man who scandalised the bankers and industrialists of the whole world by ignoring the classical economic rules. In abandoning the gold standard he flew in the face of venerable tradition and accepted the risk of inflation and a tidal wave of paper money. In London the government expressed "bitter resentment" at these policies whilst the press spoke of "Roosevelt the clown". Only the great British economist John Maynard Keynes defended him: it was a very long time, he said, since any statesman had had the nerve to brush away so many cobwebs.

And there was no shortage of cobwebs in the heads of many well-meaning people among the clergy and laity, who at just that time were calling Alberione a madman and worse. There was no end of presbytery gossip about the disastrous blunders being perpetrated by "that man".

James Alberione had certainly never met Mr Roosevelt and it is doubtful if he had ever read anything by the British professor whose ideas so horrified the practitioners of traditional finance. But it was not because he favoured the theories of either of them that he ignored the accepted rules of prudence. He simply placed his trust in "prayer, study, apostolate and poverty". These, he used to say, were the wheels that kept the Pauline wagon rolling. Even his flashes of entrepreneurial genius came to him on the spur of the moment, in the middle of his daily routine of four hours' prayer, the Four Last Things and the Spiritual Exercises of St Ignatius.

We are beginning to feel at home here

The Daughters were feeling the need for more space at Alba and Fr Alberione ordered the construction at San Cassiano of a home that they could call entirely their own. This was to be their Mother house and the sisters took it over in stages as each part became ready for occupation.

There was no heating – not even glass in the windows – when Thecla moved in with the first working party. Curtains were hung immediately and they quickly began to fit the place out with beds, tables and equipment for the kitchen. An electricity generator was installed, but every now and again they had to fall back on the supply of candles which Thecla had prudently provided. "We are beginning to feel at home here," was the comment of one of the sisters.

The move was not merely a minor adjustment to the living accommodation at Alba. Maestra Thecla began to see much less of Fr Alberione and for the first time she experienced the exaltations and miseries of ultimate responsibility. From now on the characteristic atmosphere of the household would increasingly reflect her own personal style.

The apostolate, though still in its early days, had become

an international venture and this had its impact on the whole way of life at the Mother house. In 1935 Thecla began what was to become a regular personal correspondence with all the Daughters wherever they might be working, and they in turn were expected to write to her twice a year – at Christmas and on 29 June, the feast of St Paul. Problems of community life could no longer be resolved face to face when sisters were living in Argentina, Brazil and the United States.

A religious community can truly be said to have a home of its own only when it is allowed to reserve the Holy Eucharist in a church or chapel. Furniture, fittings and equipment – even light and heating – may all be lacking, but not the Real Presence of Our Lord in the tabernacle.

So whilst they were waiting for their new church to be built, the Daughters of St Paul used a temporary building as their first chapel for perpetual adoration. At Alba in those days this was a fundamental activity for the Daughters as well as the Pious Disciples, a sign of special consecration and a spiritual power-house supporting those who worked in the field. This was how one of the sisters described the devotions as they performed them at Borgo Piave:

"Our main purpose is to give praise and glory to God... Duties are organised on a weekly basis. Each watch consists of two sisters and lasts for two hours. During day-time the watches are kept by the novices and others, whilst the professed sisters watch through the night. Prayers are always based on the theme of Jesus the Master, the Way, the Truth and the Light. The first period is devoted to readings, meditation and recitation of the joyful mysteries of the rosary; then comes examination of conscience followed by the sorrowful mysteries, and finally we pray for forgiveness and end with the glorious mysteries. Time passes so quickly that we hardly notice it. At night we kneel on the steps of the altar; during the day at the altar-rail. I have often taken my turn in the deepest hours of the night: the tabernacle would have been left open by the priest after evening

Benediction and there would be the six great candles, speaking to Jesus of our faith and casting their light over the two of us at prayer.

"Outside everything would be perfectly silent. From time to time some nocturnal wanderer might pass along the road right next to our building; we would hear him in the distance as he approached and sometimes we would tremble with fear, instinctively looking towards each other, thankful for the gratings at the windows, praying that he would go away... At the end of the third part of the Visit one of us would go and waken the two sisters of the next watch whilst the other remained behind waiting to hand over."

Naturally, the chapel was not heated; they would never have dreamed of such a thing. "In winter and the colder months we used to throw a long, warm cloak of black woollen material over our shoulders. There were two of them and we handed them on from one watch to the next." Thecla had made them with her own hands for the Daughters. She used to wear one herself when she took her turn in the prayers, readings and meditations along with the others, which she did with one addition: she could not resist bursting into song in the presence of the Lamb of God.

She often sang when she met groups of her Daughters and whilst she was travelling, whether in company or alone. And in this she was doing no more than follow the example of St Paul when he was imprisoned with Silas at Philippi. The warder "put them the inner prison and fastened their feet in the stocks. But about midnight Paul and Silas were praying and singing hymns to God..."

The construction of their elegant gothic church dedicated to the Divine Master was eventually completed and the building was consecrated in 1936.

Nothing but the best for the apostolate

"On the basis of a survey we have carried out it would seem that they go best among the professional classes –

lawyers, doctors, pharmacists and so on..." Thecla was writing to her Daughters about the various editions of the Bible. They were selling well; certainly better than might have been expected in such times.

But many years were to pass before the Ecumenical Council came out with its clear statement that the faithful must have easy access to both New and Old Testaments.

James Alberione had taken this view many years before, displaying more daring than he ever did in his lavish spending on machinery or buildings. Without backers or guarantees he put into circulation several different editions of the Bible, challenging both prejudice and ignorance with the intuition and courage of the great publisher. He was not content to wait for the right moment; he would personally work to create it.

The Daughters of St Paul were always at the disposal of this extraordinary intuition. Thecla herself taught some of the detailed techniques of persuasion. In a circular of April 1934 addressed to the houses she writes: "Present the prospective buyer with a choice of bibles in Latin and Italian, each in the single binding and in separate volumes, and get them to chose the one he likes best. When you've made your sale, get them to write something like this on a piece of paper: 'I have bought the Bible... I like it very much... I am very happy with it... It is beautifully made...' or whatever. Then you call on someone else and show them what the first buyer has written, and so on, getting everyone to write a few words, or at least to put their signature. Not everyone will agree to do this, but the majority do. Try it in Our Lord's name."

After the first difficulties, the Alba presses began to turn out extremely attractive bibles; they had an immediate appeal to many buyers because they "felt good in the hand". In fact much was changing in the organisation, though the transformation was so gradual that even those involved were scarcely aware of how far they had moved.

It was in the Thirties that they began to speak in the past

tense about things which had once seemed part of an unalterable way of life. For example, they no longer transported books and papers to the railway station in hand carts or horse-drawn wagons. One day they bought their first lorry, and this was soon followed by cars and vans.

As for printing machinery, they would no longer dream of purchasing used equipment. There might still be a few rooms with unglazed windows and many that lacked central heating, but in the printing department there was nothing but the newest and most advanced machinery. The aim of "working with the fastest and most efficient means" had already been achieved.

The problem of formation

However, not everything was going so smoothly, especially during the long years of the slump. Daughters of St Paul could not be recruited ready made; they were, and would always be, works of spiritual craftsmanship – never a machine-made product. Thecla was naturally the chief artisan in this process of formation, and as the years went by and her sisters became more scattered across the world this was done increasingly by letter and in circulars like "The Echo of the Mother house", which was started in early 1934.

There was the further problem of working out a way of life and earning a living in the book centres during the economic crisis. Some people simply could not afford to buy and others paid very slowly. There were books that almost leaped from the shelves of their own accord, whilst others – often the more rewarding titles – had to be promoted with as much effort as it cost to sell ten of the others. All these difficulties were fed back to Thecla for suggestions and solutions.

Her ability to make quick decisions was just one of her qualifications as general manager of the enterprise. But first and foremost Thecla was the "maestra," who approached every problem from the standpoint of spiritual formation, whether it concerned delivery deadlines, stock levels or sales turnover. In one of her circulars of 1932 we read: "I hear complaints from nearly all of you that people aren't paying on time, that you have debts of your own that you can't settle, that you don't know how you can possibly manage, and much more in this vein. On reflection it seems to me that the fault lies in ourselves and that we are not really doing the will of God..." She goes on to say that although it may seem a boring administrative chore to complete the weekly and monthly returns on time, especially when there is nothing new to say, these jobs must all be seen as another aspect of the will of God. If the sisters will only think of them in that way they will see a light shining through even the dreariest of clerical duties. "You can't expect to do every job equally well, but if you set about your work determined to do the holy will of God you won't fail and you will see that everything turns out for the best. You will find help coming from the most unexpected quarters and the work will be easier. Believe it! Make an act of faith now! We never have enough faith, because we always think the best way to do a thing is the one that suits us best. Isn't that really the problem?"

Again, certain books "full of sentiment but with little substance go like the wind, whilst others – the ones with a deeper message – gather dust in the stock-room." Thecla's reaction illustrates the difference between religious and commercial publishing, between dedication and mere professionalism: "The books that are left are often those that may do the most good. So if people don't look at them it is up to us to point them out. Isn't it our mission to bring the Word of God to those who are not actually looking for it?"

A difficult message; but then no one had promised easy payments or cut prices to these women when they consecrated themselves to God. Nevertheless they are words full of wisdom, though Thecla may not have known that she was echoing the thoughts of the Greek philosophers and of the Fathers of the Church. In her letters she taught from her own experience, drawing on home-grown qualifications. She urged her sisters to aim at self-realisation based on co-operation with the action of God's grace within each of them. The apostolate of the printed word would not be advanced by a mere flurry of activity. On the contrary, the Daughters must abandon themselves to God in full simplicity and strive to become more perfect as his instruments, more amenable to his purposes. As St Paul says in his Epistle to the Romans: "Likewise the Spirit helps us in our weakness; for we do not know how to pray as we ought, but the Spirit himself intercedes for us with sighs too deep for words." (Rom 8:26)

She matured and grew in stature over the years as a spiritual guide and teacher though without ever climbing, as it were, into the pulpit – quite the contrary. If she had occasion to write something of particular importance she would often show it to one of her sisters for possible amendments before it was issued. And she had none of that mannered solemnity – innocent enough in itself – which characterised the speech of so many senior religious of her day. Mothers general, women of undoubted holiness, used to speak and write in the manner of the more notable preachers of the day, filling out their sentences with Latin quotations and stilted metaphors. Thecla's words were always simple and homespun, with examples drawn from her own down-to-earth background.

In short she knew how to remain herself, keeping fresh that inborn good sense which led her to distrust excessive fervour and to identify most easily with those who felt distressed, weak or inadequate. She never demanded instant results and was understanding with anyone who tried and failed.

The two things she would not tolerate were weakness of will and spiritual laziness. Here compromise was impossible and she was quick to put offenders in mind of the Four Last Things. Every day, she would remind them, the work we do – for better or worse – counts towards our own eternal reward. In this matter there can be no place for anything less than a wholehearted quest for virtue and a readiness for total sacrifice. Whenever she sensed compromise in the air Thecla spoke with unambiguous clarity, ever ready to point out "the blandishments of the devil", to fight laziness or lack of faith even in small things. Not even the special circumstances arising from the apostolate of the press could justify certain failings, for the first duty of the Daughters of St Paul, as of all religious families, is personal holiness.

Fr Alberione develops the same thought in a letter of 1933 to Maestra Thecla: "The Daughters must place a lot more faith in Our Lord than they do in themselves; otherwise they will exhaust their energies, whilst they need to be healthy and strong. The apostolate is indeed their specific task, but it is the secondary object of the Congregation; they ought not to make themselves ill with it. Our Lord will see their faith and their right intentions and from these will flow great results."

So wrote James Alberione, and on that occasion Thecla was scrupulous in passing on his words. But on others her style and timing were different enough to make us wonder how far the normally most obedient Prima Maestra was taking her lead from the Founder and how far she was expressing her own mind.

Visits to the overseas houses

Her intense and regular correspondence with the far-flung houses was extremely useful but it was not enough. She had to travel to maintain proper contact with the work of the Congregation – to see things for herself, to speak to her sisters, and to listen to their experiences – and so she made two transatlantic journeys in as many years. She had already travelled widely in Italy, but it was quite a different matter to visit the totally different world of the Americas and to bring encouragement to Daughters who had lived away from Alba for so long.

On 26 March 1936 she left for South America from Genoa on the liner *Augustus*, Fr Alberione having decided that she should travel unaccompanied. It was a great distance for a maiden voyage and even more difficult for a woman with a delicate constitution, though fortunately she was spared the agonies of sea-sickness.

It cannot have been an easy experience to find herself quite alone to face the sudden withdrawal from the rhythms of community's daily routine. But as already mentioned she adapted herself calmly to novelty and inconvenience.

She arrived in São Paulo on 3 April to find a newly installed printing press at work. It was a very small operation, but it was already producing *A Familia Crista*, a periodical destined to enjoy a long life. Moreover the Daughters had found a home, opened a book centre, and were about to take the momentous step of buying a plot of land to build a larger permanent house with a noviciate, for the first vocations were beginning to appear.

The Prima Maestra sailed on from Santos for Argentina on 3 June. Here the sisters' problems had taken longer to resolve, but by 1933 they had been able to set to work with the usual start-up equipment of platen press, guillotine and stitching machine. Here too they had established a popular periodical dealing with religious instruction called *Il Buon Angelo*. As in the other two American missions, the first sisters to arrive had now been joined by further recruits from Italy; but there were also a few Argentinean girls about the house, lending a hand and becoming interested in the wider purpose of the mission. The prospects for local vocations were good. The house at that time was hardly suitable to accommodate a noviciate but the Daughters had already seen premises outside Buenos Aires which would be ideal.

Thecla was quick to note the very different world which confronted the Daughters. She wrote about her impressions to the sisters in Italy, particularly about one reaction for which she, with her European perspectives, was quite unprepared. "Here they speak about 'Europe', about 'Europeans', about 'leaving for Europe'. It comes as a shock." Again, using a language very much of its period, she talks about some of the things that have struck her in the New World. "The whole atmosphere of Latin America is extremely corrupt. Those who do not come from a very solid background quickly lose the faith. You find Russians, Germans, Turks, Jews and Protestants, but the Italians make up the largest community among the immigrants. They are not much different from the rest. However there are some good Catholics here as well as some very beautiful churches. The Buenos Aires Eucharistic Congress [of 1934] has done much good and everyone remembers it with great pleasure. There is good in this place, but also so much evil. The devil works without ceasing. All the people I have spoken to say that the press is the answer, our own press, our chosen apostolate. Just think, there is a publisher here who produces a newspaper devoted to witchcraft and which carries the image of Satan on its masthead. And it is quite legal. The sisters do what they can, accepting great sacrifices in the middle of enormous difficulties."

Having described the situation with her habitual realism, she immediately proceeds to indicate what should be done about it: not better organisation, more machinery or investment – certainly not! In difficult situations "what is needed is that every sister should learn detachment from her own wilfulness and cultivate the habit of self-sacrifice." This was where Thecla wanted the investment – in the spiritual quality of the Daughters of St Paul, by instilling in them the basic Christian paradox that conquest comes through self-denial.

She now knew how much there was to accomplish in the Americas; it was a limitless task, but the first priority for every Daughter was that she should live "not for this life, but for eternity; not for this world but for heaven". So the apostolate of the printed word saw growth and development – Thecla never spoke of success – even in these inhospitable lands.

Finally she landed at New York. This had been the most difficult of the missions, involving the longest wait in a situation of canonical irregularity, reluctantly tolerated by the local authorities. But the struggle had been won; Cardinal Hayes had been persuaded by the stubbornness of the sisters themselves, the help of the Pauline priests and the support of the Italian American, Mgr Gaetano Arcesi. Reinforcements were sent out immediately. At first their activities had been confined to the Italian immigrant population, but as their knowledge of English improved the range of their activities became progressively wider.

Maestra Thecla found the tiny community living in rented accommodation on Byron Avenue, in the Bronx. They now had legitimate domicile there and they had even received their first American postulant. But the place was minute; they needed more room, and on a freehold basis if possible. Thecla was immediately taken by this city of New York and by the American people, and decided to come back as soon as she could. She wanted to do everything possible to help the Daughters establish their new house, for which a loan had been negotiated. She returned from this first visit on the *Conte Biancamano*, landing at Genoa on 27 August 1936. She was back at Alba two days later, and no sooner had she set foot in the Mother house than she led the sisters into church to give thanks to God in her favourite way, by raising her voice in song. So began a tradition: from then onwards she concluded all her journeys with the *Magnificat*.

The Rex *is tossed in an Atlantic storm*

Thecla began her second journey to the United States at the end of January 1937, arriving on 4 February. She set off home again on 27 February, landing at Naples and arriving in Rome on 6 March. The New York community of the Daughters would now have a house of its own on Staten Island, linked to the city by a ferry, on which the sisters became habitual and popular commuters. In addition to distributing their books they often collected clothes for the missions, so that their bags were usually full on both outward and inward journeys.

So Thecla's journey was brief. She also travelled at speed – on the *Rex*, at 51,000 tons and nearly 800 feet long, the most prestigious transatlantic liner of its day and the pride of the Italian merchant fleet. From 1933 to 1935 it held the "blue riband" for the fastest crossing of the Atlantic. But there was a surprise in store on this occasion for the ocean was unusually rough. She described her ordeal to the Daughters: "Imagine a vessel as huge as the *Rex* being thrown about by the waves like a twig. One moment it is hurled up onto a crest, the next it crashes down into a trough; then it is thrown to the side, writhing, creaking and groaning as though it were held in the jaws of a vice. It is an absolutely terrifying experience, and it certainly concentrates the mind."

Before leaving she had said nothing about this voyage to her family at Castagnito so as to avoid worrying them. She begged their pardon when she got back to Rome in a letter to "parents, brothers, sisters-in-law, nephews and nieces", in which she tells them all about her voyage and the furies of the Atlantic. She is careful to put their minds at rest: "I didn't suffer at all. Everyone was quite amazed, and called me a great sailor – 'the heroine of the sea'. Just imagine! Nearly all the passengers were in bed with sea-sickness whilst I stayed up the whole time and never lost a meal."

In the February-March 1937 issue of "Echo of the Mother house" under the title "What I have learned" Thecla summarised her conclusions from the two American journeys. There we find confirmation of her fundamental certainties, enriched now by this first overseas experience. We see too the re-emergence of many ideas, strengthened by trial in the field, which are not new to the Pauline spirituality.

She begins very firmly: "In everything, whether we like it or not, we must look first for the will of God and accept it calmly, without worry. In short we must accept everything from the hands of God, our Good Father." Then she urges them to reflect: "We shall never be able to thank Our Lord enough for the great grace of a vocation. Our vocation in the Daughters of St Paul is so great and so beautiful that we shall not understand it fully until we get to heaven." And on the problem of study: "When you have travelled the world a bit you understand better how much more good can be done when knowledge and virtue work together. Give special importance to the catechism, as you were taught in the house." So the sisters are encouraged to persevere in their studies so that they become better at communicating with others and thus more effective in the apostolate.

But she warns anyone whose devotion to study tempts them into undue self-esteem or presumption: "That it is Our Lord who does everything; our task is to remove whatever obstacles stand in his way, meaning our love of self and of our own point of view... That unless we deny ourselves we shall not be able to achieve anything, for all around us and at all times there are opportunities for doing penance... That it is easy to lose heart when we do not mortify the mind, the imagination and the heart. We must never cease trying to remove the 'me' from our thoughts so that God may reign."

Let us look again to the idea of knowledge and virtue working together. It was not just one precept among many but the very essence of her method as a spiritual teacher, and one that she fully shared with the Founder. For the Daughters of St Paul education was not simply an intellectual ornament; it was a duty to the Congregation. Without their studies they could not consider themselves completely formed; they could not meet the demands of such an exacting vocation as the apostolate of the press, where they would be called on to write as well as to print and distribute the work of others. Fr Alberione insisted that they should make every effort to prepare themselves through study for the editorial function. The example of the first editor of *Famiglia Cristiana* was later followed, after years of study, by many others.

Thecla eagerly supported the Founder's wishes for she was well aware of the pressing need for a firm educational grounding for the Daughters. Canon Chiesa's school taught them many things, but it also instilled in them a keen desire to learn more and to study in greater depth. She herself had taken every opportunity, through lessons, courses and conferences, of making progress in this direction. Some of the sisters asked to pursue their religious studies at a higher level so that they could meet this urgent request from Fr Alberione: "It is essential for the Daughters of St Paul to have an education equal to the challenge of their mission; their first objective should be a mastery of editorial skills."

The Prima Maestra devoted herself to this task with her customary singleness of mind: the Congregation needed sisters who could write well, so an immediate start had to be made on training them. "Editorial work is the hardest part of our apostolate. Let us pray for those who are being prepared for this task, that they may succeed."

Already in 1931-2 there had been a course of religious studies, though it had been conducted as an unofficial experiment with only a few students. The first regular courses in philosophy and theology began in 1934, which began and concluded with particular solemnity. Maestra Thecla occasionally sat in on the lectures so as not to lose sight of her students. At the beginning of the 1935 session she summed up in three points the obligations that they had undertaken: "1) Those who study must do so with the right disposition, namely to devote themselves to the glory of God and for the good of souls; otherwise they will not succeed; 2) they must have trust in Our Lord so that by studying for one hour they will learn for four – as in 'the Pact, or secret of success'; 3) they must recognise the sisters who teach them as the bearers of the words of Our Lord."

The decisive importance of Thecla's contribution to the development of these studies among the Daughters was solemnly underlined by Fr Alberione when he wrote: "She was a constant help to me in the preparation of the Daughters of St Paul for their special apostolate. It was a most unusual initiative for those times and by human standards a difficult one; but under her guidance writers, speakers, technicians and propagandists were educated, as well as radio and film technicians of every kind." The quotation is from *Abundantes Divitiae* (How infinitely rich is his grace!), a collection of notes on the charism of the Pauline family written by Fr Alberione on the occasion of the fortieth anniversary of the foundation of the Society of St Paul.

The Eternal City in time of war

Bishop Re of Alba, died early in 1933 and in the summer Luigi Maria Grassi of Mondovì, a religious of the Barnabite Fathers, was consecrated as his successor; he was a fearless man of God who was to attract wider notice during the dark days of the second World War. During his time as bishop of Alba the Society passed beyond the pioneering stage and began to expand overseas with furious energy: indeed in 1934 and 1935 Fr Alberione sent priests and brothers of the Society, all more or less empty-handed, to establish houses in Spain, Poland, India, Japan and the Philippines.

Another important development was the Primo Maestro's decision in June 1936 to move to Rome, taking up residence in the house in Via Grottaperfetta, whilst Fr Giaccardo returned to Alba as local superior of the men's Congregation, though still reporting directly to Fr Alberione. In November of the same year Thecla followed the Founder from Alba to Rome to set up the Generalate or General house of the Daughters in Via Grottaperfetta. Later, the noviciate and the house of studies for those following courses in theology and philosophy were also established in the Eternal City. One of the advantages of the new arrangements was that the Daughters now had access to the great Roman libraries, ecclesiastic and lay. In this way the headquarters of the Pauline family were established within easy reach of those Roman authorities which would be of fundamental importance for its future.

Another green shoot

In Rome Fr Alberione had another surprise for Thecla in the form of a completely new congregation, the Sisters of Jesus the Good Shepherd, also known as the *Pastorelle*. Two Daughters were needed to start this new organisation, and Alberione had already chosen one of these himself. This community was to have a range of purposes: preparing sisters to help with pastoral work in the parishes – from the teaching of catechism to participation in Catholic Action, helping in infants' schools, organising work projects for young girls and helping the disabled to take a fuller part in the liturgy. It was another example of "the involvement of women in the holy mission of the priesthood", which brought new ideas into a traditional role, including many of specifically Pauline inspiration such as educational activities, the use of books, newspapers, radio, slides and other aids.

It was an attractive idea which reflected his wish to contribute something to every aspect of the life of the Church. But to provide sisters for a new venture was no simple matter when there were not even enough of them to meet existing obligations. The Founder seems to have offered little by way of explanation or assistance, and Thecla could not have expected anything more. He had come to assume she would always understand. And her obedience did indeed perform the usual miracle. She announced the new foundation to the Daughters with these words of encouragement: "Let us study their programme carefully and then set to work to find vocations for this new Pauline organisation which will devote itself to pastoral activities." This was in April 1937, and two months later she was repeating the request for "a special effort for vocations, particularly for the family of the Good Shepherd; this work is especially pleasing to Our Lord".

After a year of preparation under the personal supervision of Fr Alberione the new community found a home at Genzano, some 25 miles south of Rome, and in 1938, true to his established custom in financial matters, the Founder bade them farewell as they left with just 100 Lire. Thecla was also there to see them off. She approached the group almost furtively – as though she were stealing rather than giving – and handed them another 200 Lire, some bread and a salami.

She followed their later career from a discreet distance and when needed she offered a tactful word of advice, wrote a short letter or paid them a brief visit. She also lent some of the Daughters to help them with formation and studies, especially as examinations approached. One of them was later to testify: "We were in no doubt that the Prima Maestra loved us dearly. In one of her notes she wrote to us, 'I am following all the wonderful things that you're doing and they give me great pleasure. May the Lord be praised.'"

Her affection was returned and in 1938 during a period of unusually poor health Thecla spent a period of convalescence with them at Genzano.

The long march to the East

The year 1937 was an important one in the history of the Daughters of St Paul for other reasons. Their missionary thrust was gathering speed along with that of their male colleagues, and in the East both communities came into collision with events that were about to change the whole world.

On 8 January 1937 the Daughters at Alba watched the departure of three of their companions, Edvige Soldano,

Elena Ramondetti and Maria Cleofe Zanoni. They were setting out on an even more extraordinary adventure than the first journey to the Americas. Their destination was China, where they would find a small number of men of the Society who had arrived in 1934.

It was a time of extraordinary events in that country: the army of Generalissimo Chiang Kai-shek, the main support of the nationalist government, had made peace and formed an alliance with the revolutionary communist forces of Mao Tse-tung. Having fought almost to the death, the two armies decided to unite in order to throw the Japanese out of Manchuria and large areas of China. The occupation of these territories was one of the consequences of the "Treaties of Shame" which Imperial China had been forced to sign by the Western powers and Japan after the Boxer Rising at the beginning of the century. According to the treaties, the regiments of the Rising Sun were in China to guarantee communications between Peking and the coast, thus protecting the route for Japanese imports, which competed ruthlessly with home-produced goods.

About the same time there occurred in Tokyo the so-called "26 February incident", a military coup aimed at destroying the power of the "corrupt intriguers" by physically eliminating the entire government. The conspirators succeeded in killing the Minister of Finance and a few senior officials, but they completely missed their chief target, Prime Minister Keisuke Okada, murdering his brother-in-law by mistake. The turmoil finally subsided after two government crises and the execution by firing squad of several of the rebels. At last, in June the 47-year-old Prince Fumimaro Koyone came to power at the head of a government which promised reforms, constitutional progress and peace.

The three Daughters of St Paul travelled out during the month of January, and on landing at Hangchow they were met by the men of the Society, who had arrived two years before and had begun a small printing operation. They had intended to make their base at Hangchow, but Bishop Yu Pin of Nanking and a future cardinal, invited them to establish themselves in his city, which at the time was also the capital. So the two communities of the Pauline family were travelling companions as they sailed slowly up the Yangtze, arriving at Nanking on Good Friday. The printing machinery followed after Easter and Fr Alberione's men were soon able to begin work again. The Daughters were meanwhile installed in a small house, where they began to study the language.

But on 7 July 1937, about 20 miles from Peking at the old stone Marco Polo bridge, there occurred a trivial incident which was to have momentous repercussions. Chinese troops fired on a detachment of Japanese soldiers engaged in a training exercise. There were explanations and apologies and the episode seemed to be closed, but within the next few days there was more shooting and mutual recriminations. At this point the two high commands became involved in the argument and on 27 July, after negotiations characterised by genuine misunderstandings and some bad faith, Prime Minister Konoye announced from Tokyo that the Japanese troops in China were being deployed to create a "new order" in East Asia.

Though it was announced as a large scale police operation, in reality it was a declaration of war against China and a first step towards the wider hostilities to come. The Japanese bombers attacked Chinese cities and the invading divisions of the Rising Sun advanced. Within a few weeks both Shanghai and Nanking had been occupied, and thirty million refugees dispersed in all directions along roads and rivers or across the fields, pushing their hand-carts, shouldering their bundles, carrying their children. Somewhere in this sea of humanity, having lost contact with the members of the men's Congregation, were Edvige, Elena and Maria Cleofe.

So began the "Long March" of the three Daughters of St Paul. They tried in vain to reach Shanghai and then failed to get back to Nanking. But eventually, expelled by the authorities of the "new order", they were forced to seek shelter beyond the borders of China. They were now totally isolated in the middle of the most densely populated country in the world. They had no news of the men of the Society, who were likewise unable to make contact either with them or with Italy. Back in Rome, Thecla knew only that there was war in China; there was nothing she could do for the three missing Daughters but pray.

Travelling by road and river the three eventually succeeded in reaching Hong Kong and from there they set off for India, where the Society had a house in the capital, New Delhi. When they arrived however it was only to hear that their presence was unwelcome – indeed extremely unwelcome, for the men themselves were barely tolerated by the Archbishop of Delhi, who was actively trying to get rid of them. He absolutely refused to accept the Daughters, even on a provisional basis. So Edvige, Elena and Maria Cleofe had once again to find somewhere to go – and as soon as possible.

From India they had at least been able to get in touch with Maestra Thecla in Rome, but this was not to ask whether they might return home; they wanted to know where else she wanted to send them. The reply was not long in coming: they were to proceed to the Philippines, where a well-established house of the Society was ready to give all the necessary help and where the local archbishop was not unsympathetic to the presence of foreign nuns. They left Delhi without regrets and they took ship from Bombay, reaching the end of their odyssey at Manila on 13 October 1938.

For the first two months the sisters found a comfortable home with the Benedictine nuns of the College of St Scholastica. There they recovered from the rigours of their several journeys and rebuilt their strength. Then in early December they moved to Lipa in the province of Batangas, where the men of the Society had a house. And so, driven there by war, expulsions and months of wandering, the Sisters of St Paul began their mission in the Philippines.

From the treasury of her heart

In a letter of 1937 to her parents Thecla asked for news about a book on agriculture that she used to read at home in the early days of the century. She needed it, she said, so that she could make arrangements for the proper cultivation of the fertile land round the General house and perhaps to start keeping bees. Whatever she came across in life she always tried, if possible, to put it to use in the service of the Institute. Not to do so was for her like throwing something away, a sinful waste as well as a breach of the vow of poverty. When Fr Alberione taught her that this virtue consisted of five functions, "to renounce, to produce, to preserve, to provide and to edify", he meant that the practice of poverty and unremitting hard work were part and parcel of the same concept – making the best use of your time. He himself used to make a point on his travels of never visiting famous basilicas, ancient abbeys and the like. He considered that kind of thing a distraction and a waste of time. He considered it far more important to press on and arrive early at your destination.

Not so Thecla, who loved experiences of this kind and was keen that others should appreciate them as occasions of pure joy and spiritual consolation. For her, a monument, religious or secular, a spectacular natural phenomenon or a beautiful view was an occasion to pause and to share her reactions and emotions with the Daughters, and often to make some subtle connection with the supernatural. Occasionally she would break into song. She had special love of the jubilant praise of Psalm 148: "Praise the Lord! Praise the Lord from the heavens, praise him in the heights... Praise him, sun and moon, praise him all you shining stars!..."

As already mentioned, Fr Alberione warned the Daughters about the dangers of over-work: they should live for their mission, not make themselves ill with it. And Thecla followed up this exhortation with more detailed suggestions. For example in one of her circulars of 1938 we find this : "There is one piece of advice that I must give you and it is this, that you look after your health and do your best to avoid illness. First of all you must take all the common-sense precautions and observe the elementary rules of medicine. In summer it is a good idea to get up half an hour later and eat plenty of fruit, particularly cooked fruit. Remember also, whenever you need it, to take a tonic. In this way you will avoid those small discomforts and so many minor illnesses."

In 1938 the "grape cure" was widely recommended and grape-harvest festivals of various kinds were held all over Italy. Another "fruit in season" was the new rule of the Fascist regime which banned the traditional word for "you", used when addressing anyone except family and close friends. It was to be replaced with the plural form, as in French. In the same circular Thecla suggests to the Daughters that they would do well to avoid problems by observing the new regulation – and without making too much fuss about it.

Their own publishing house

There was one problem that had been with the Congregation from the beginning but which only now came to the surface after the first period of consolidation. Was it enough for the Daughters to confine themselves to printing and distributing books and periodicals? In a circular of December 1938 the Prima Maestra announced that the time had come to tackle what had so far seemed an unrealisable objective. Since Fr Alberione had first conceived the Daughters of St Paul as a religious family and also as "teaching institutes" it was time they extended their activities to cover writing. Thecla continued: "We must now devote all our energies and concentrate our efforts on this. In order to centralise all our editorial, printing and distribution efforts on behalf of our own titles the Primo Maestro has laid down a policy which we must follow faithfully... As a first step every book centre should now rearrange its window display, substituting our own publications for those of other publishers. The displays must be tasteful and show a suitable variety of titles. It is a good idea to give the best position in the window to the Holy Bible or the Gospels and to arrange the other books around them."

Naturally enough, the Founder made sure that Thecla herself was among the first to be involved in the process of self-improvement through study. The lessons in dogmatic and moral theology given at Alba by Canon Chiesa had been an exceptional educational opportunity for her and the other pioneers. But now the process was to be taken a further stage by allowing suitable members of the community to embark on regular higher studies. They were to become writers, journalists and editors of periodicals and books. And those studies opened up the prospect of a further precious task: the education of priests, brothers, laymen, groups and communities in the whole field of social communication. So these sisters were to become familiar with the different worlds of newspapers, books, radio, the cinema and the organisation of cultural events to compensate for the inexperience of the clergy, who rarely had any proper training in these matters.

The phenomenon of the cinema took bishops and priests by surprise, though they soon became keen to make use of it. But they felt ill at ease in the culture of moving pictures; they saw it as a rather hostile environment. To understand it they needed to be led by the hand through its complications and to learn to trust it. And there, in the book centres of the Daughters of St Paul, were women who had received formal training in this field and were keen to help. In this way the book centres became a first point of contact for the clergy who wanted to explore the new technology as a further means of evangelisation.

"Study", writes Sister Lorenzina Guidetti of the Daughters of St Paul, "must always be directed towards the apostolate; it is not an end in itself. [Maestra Thecla] used to urge us to humility, faith in Our Lord and gratitude to the Congregation: 'Whilst you are studying your sisters are working for you. Not every one receives the grace to be able to study... Remember that those who study also have the greater responsibility.'"

From time to time Thecla, through no fault of her own, would find herself attracting the strong disapproval of individual bishops, who might even forbid the sisters to bring books and newspapers into their dioceses. This situation usually arose from complaints by parish priests about the excessive zeal of some of her younger nuns – small vexations which nevertheless had to be dealt with.

Perhaps some Daughters might try to sell books in a diocese which had already been assigned to others. It was not the end of the world, but Thecla took care to send out a circular requiring everyone to confine their activities to their allocated territories. She well understood how these things came to happen: "We go here because it's on the way and we pass straight through; there because we have a relative; the other place because a friend lives there; and so the house that is supposed to cover that territory, not knowing anything about all this, sends other sisters..." It was no more than a minor indiscipline, but there were always people ready to make mountains out of molehills. "People get tired of being called on and complain to the parish priest, and he may then refer it to the bishop. We have already been banned from several dioceses this year because people think we call too often."

She returned frequently to this subject, writing repeated circulars, and it might look as though she was paying too much attention to what was, after all, a fairly small matter. But we do well to take note when she considers a thing important because it reveals her most original and personal ideas – in this case her concern for the people she is trying to reach with the word of God. When she was training her sisters, Thecla always kept in mind the impression they would make as they called at the home or served in the book centres. For her, if the Daughters irritated people by contacting them too frequently it was a sign of insufficient love, or at least a lack of consideration.

Time and again in her teaching she returned to the way people were to be addressed and how they should be dealt with in the book centres. The spreading of the Word was the highest form of service but the method and style used had to be in harmony with it. It was rather like the multiplication of the loaves. Jesus performed this amazing miracle, firstly, to give a sign to the crowd who had been listening to him; but before demonstrating his power he gave proof of his consideration by inviting them to sit down on the grass.

And so all those hungry people and beggars became Jesus' guests, and the apostles their servants. That was how Thecla saw their mission across Italy and around the world, and she lost no chance of passing the message on to the Daughters: "Promotion is not just a matter of picking up a case of books and going on your rounds; you have to draw near to people and study their needs." They had not to be put off by customs, behaviour or attitudes which might be very different from those they were used to. They must, as it were, "invite them to sit down" and put them at their ease. Only in this way would the Daughters of St Paul show that they were seeking their good and working for their salvation.

If the element of courtesy is missing, everything is reduced to lists of orders, financial returns and embarrassing comparisons between the commercial performances of different parts of the organisation. When that happens discouragement, disappointment and dissatisfaction gain the upper hand. Already in 1928 Thecla had given her definition of the style and substance of this attitude: "To work with the spirit of the priest."

Chapter Five

EVERYONE AT THEIR POST

"What a joy to find myself face to face with Jesus' representative on earth! [The Pope] is tall and slim, and looks a bit like our parish priest when he was younger." She was writing to her family about her first meeting with Pius XII, and it was typical of her to connect an exceptional event with her roots at Castagnito. This happened on 7 May 1940, on the occasion of the festivities for the canonisation of the first saint to die in the twentieth century, Gemma Galgani, a young women from Lucca in central Italy. Gemma's mystical experiences had provoked lively discussion, and even bitter controversy, among believers and agnostics alike at a time when positivism was in the ascendant. Mother Gemma Giannini, who founded the Sisters of St Gemma, and had been very close to the holy woman, had wanted Maestra Thecla to be with her at the papal audience. Thecla found herself completely at ease in the presence of the Pontiff, as though in her own family. Her letter to her family continues: "I was more intimidated by the guards and all those monsignors moving about the great halls than by the Holy Father himself."

Caught up in the World War

Note the date of this meeting, 7 May 1940. Hostilities had begun nine months earlier with the invasion of Poland by Germany and later by Russia. The French and the English had declared war against Hitler's Germany.

Italy, though an ally of Germany, was still non-belligerent; but in fact there was little more than a month of peace left for the country. On the same day that Thecla was at the Vatican, the final hope faded for Italy to stand clear of the conflict. The French prime minister, Paul Reynaud, proposed negotiations to avoid hostilities between the two countries; Rome refused, and by 10 June Italy was at war.

Already in September 1939 the Daughters of St Paul had received clear and timely orders from their Mother General. In a brief circular Thecla gave three instructions: to keep calm and have faith in Our Lord; to stay at their posts and carry on with the apostolate as far as possible, and to pray for peace.

By the end of 1940 Italy had become actively engaged in hostilities, and Thecla's circular of November-December reminded the Daughters that the sacrifices imposed on them by wartime conditions amounted to nothing more than they had already accepted in their vow of poverty – another reason for continuing to observe it faithfully.

Her practical sense led her to make further suggestions. It was time to make severe economies with clothing and in the furnishing of the houses; the only real essential was to eat enough to carry on working. It was also an opportunity to show sisterly solidarity with all those who were suffering because of the war. The circular continues: "In these times of general deprivation, let us show that we too know how to share in it and to do without things, especially those that we find hardest to give up... Let us accept our own portion of the great sadness that afflicts the world."

"Stay at your posts!" This was Fr Alberione's order to all the members of the Pauline family, men and women, priests and brothers, wherever they might be. Without exception, everyone did so, despite the fact that several houses did not receive the order, owing to the breakdown of communications with the General house. This was a battle won by the Pauline family *en bloc*.

So everyone stayed on duty, starting with those in Poland, the first country to be affected by the war, and where Fr Tarcisio Ravina was arrested and subjected to a period of forced re-education by the communist invaders. In India, then part of the British Empire, Italy's entry into the war led to the arrest of Fr Alfonso Ferrero, who, owing to a misunderstanding, had been pointed out as a spy. Long months passed before the matter was cleared up, during which time Brother Bernardino Ruffoli was also imprisoned in Bombay. In the end they were interned as "enemy aliens".

In France the Daughters of St Paul had been well established near Lyons in 1935. On the outbreak of war, the Italian consulate had advised them to go back home. They stayed.

The sisters who had taken refuge in the Philippines from the chaos in China were subsequently joined by others; they had learned the language and had begun their work. They were becoming known in every town and village in the province of Batangas when the Japanese invaded. The town of Lipa was bombed to rubble and they had to abandon their house with its stock of gospels and catechisms. From that moment until the end of hostilities the Daughters of St Paul suffered the hunger and deprivations of war refugees like any other women in the Philippines.

These are just a few examples of how the men and women of the Pauline family were affected by the greatest cataclysm of the century and of how they managed to survive. There must have been times when they sensed the almost physical presence of their persecuted patron and recalled the trials that he listed in his second letter to the Christians of Corinth: "... on frequent journeys, in danger from rivers, danger from robbers, danger from my own people, danger from the Gentiles, danger in the city, danger in the wilderness, danger at sea, danger from false brethren; in toil and hardship, through many a sleepless night, in hunger and thirst, often without food, in cold and exposure." (2 Cor 11:26-27)

To see them all reappear safe and sound at the end of the war – with the first letters, the first radio reports, the first returns to Rome – must have seemed like a miracle. But more important by far than the fact of survival was their individual and collective demonstration of perseverance, despite all persecutions and temptations, and in the most diverse situations. No sooner had the echo of the last cannon faded away than news began to arrive at the Mother house from all sides that everything was in more or less working order again. No one wasted time in celebrations; they were already reaching "forward towards the finishing line" (Phil 3:13-14), as the Founder had always taught.

The sanctuary of the Queen of the Apostles

Throughout the war Fr Alberione managed to maintain that unshakeable calm which was so much a part of his character. It seemed at times that he was able to interpret the events of the conflict by means of his own private code, and to discover in them precise messages and meanings for the Pauline family. In a letter to the Pauline Cooperators in December 1940 he writes: "The most beautiful works have been realised during the most difficult periods of history. This is a matter of fact, and it gives the life to those who lose heart when faced with painful events."

Alberione went further: one day during the war he made a vow to build a majestic church close to the Generalate houses in Rome as soon as hostilities ceased. It was to be dedicated to Our Lady Queen of Apostles and would form the heart of the Pauline citadel.

Truth to tell, he had been thinking about such a project for a number of years; but Fr Giuseppe Barbero tells us: "The war gave new impetus and a stronger sense of commitment to a project which had already been postponed a number of times. There was a greater resolve because this time Fr Alberione had made a *vow* in the name of all members of the Pauline family scattered across the whole world."

The Daughters were to make a most important contribution over a long period to this enterprise, encouraged as always by Maestra Thecla. Meanwhile, amongst all her other duties in the Community, she was fighting her own war. No communiqués followed her battles, nor were there any casualties. Indeed hers was a continuous struggle to save victims from all the consequences of war: from the effects of bombs and bullets, but also from hunger and despair. As Alberione wrote to the Co-operators, some of the Prima Maestra's most beautiful achievements date from the war years.

Benedictine sisters at the Generalate

There were several hundred Daughters of St Paul scattered about Italy and dozens more were spread across the globe. Several of these were in countries far from the battlefields, whilst others were caught up in the middle of the conflict. Italy itself soon became a war zone: aerial bombardment brought everyone into the front line. This was certainly true of the house in Cagliari, on the island of Sardinia, which received a direct hit, and the sisters found themselves huddled precariously on an upper landing staring down at the rubble many feet below.

The General house in Rome was also in the front line, but luckily there were caves nearby which made excellent air raid shelters. Thecla radiated a contagious calm in this challenging situation and showed herself a true leader with an intuitive grasp of what needed to be done in that sea of disorder. By letter and word of mouth, by telephone and in notes carried by hand she remained in touch with most of her communities. She always stressed two points: firstly, the sisters were never to ignore the common-sense rules of personal safety, and secondly, they must never be afraid of anything or of anybody.

It was advice she confirmed by her own daily example. This is how she struck Giuseppe Zilli, a future editor of *Famiglia Cristiana*, who often observed her during those frequent nocturnal dashes for shelter: "She never seemed worried, always calm and relaxed. She looked as if she had always lived within a higher scheme of things. I don't know if the Prima Maestra had much schooling, but I always got the impression of being in the presence of an exceptionally wise woman, quite lacking in affectation."

It would have been understandable if war-time conditions had led to some loss of heart or spiritual weariness among the communities, justifying the relaxation of a regime which could have seemed less relevant to a changed world. Thecla was alive to this temptation and left the Daughters in no doubt that the apostolate was to continue. It might call for new methods according to the time and place, but the commitment must remain absolutely firm.

Looking through her circulars of the war years, we find the usual operational instructions about deadlines, overdue payments, scholarships and similar matters – more or less as in peace-time; and of course she insists that her sisters continue to look for vocations. Both she and Alberione were already thinking about the trained recruits who would be needed as soon as the fighting was over.

So there was no excuse for reduced effort. Indeed the war was continually present in Thecla's thoughts in terms of what it demanded of Christians and consecrated women; and according to the austere teaching of the Prima Maestra the times demanded a great deal. One of her circulars even urged the sisters to show self-control in the face of misfortunes to members of their families: "Sometimes there is no end to weeping and moaning, and this is not a good thing: it is not fitting behaviour for a nun. And on the subject of pain, I should like us all to reflect rather more on the fact that we have very little to endure compared with so many people."

The Daughters of St Paul ought rather to be the consolers of their families. In another circular she urges them "to write more frequently to relatives who have sons in the forces, and to write every two weeks to their brothers at the front. These letters will bring them comfort and a spirit of acceptance and of faith." Her own father Ettore Merlo died at Castagnito on 9 March 1941, but she could not travel north to console her mother, and it was not until August, during a visit to Alba, that she was at last able to see her family. She was happy that her mother had gone to Barolo to stay in the presbytery of her son Fr Leone.

Back in Rome Thecla cared for certain members of the "silent poor", people who were hungry but were too proud to talk about their plight. For example, there were three women of noble family who had managed to conceal their wretchedness from everyone but her. She was glad to be able to bring them help in secret and, as one of her sisters recalls, "she used to sing to herself as he made up the parcels".

There were other front lines for the Daughters. For example in 1944 a young member of the Congregation was dying of tuberculosis in a sanatorium in the Veneto region, and lay in the grip of despair as death approached. Thecla left for the north, heedless of the dangers, as soon as she heard of the situation. Sister Nazarena Morando gives this account of their meeting: "[The Prima Maestra] spoke to her in that motherly way of hers, radiating a faith that filled the heart... By the end of their long conversation the sister was utterly transformed... The approach of death held no more terrors for her; indeed she was calmly resigned to die there and then if that was the will of God."

Accounts of the war years recall stories of more ancient conflicts, when those least able to defend themselves were reduced to begging from door to door. One thinks of the times of St Benedict, with the wars between Goths and Byzantines, when the starving wandered the countryside and fugitives sought shelter in woods and caves. Fourteen centuries later Thecla found herself dealing with similar misfortunes – the same wretchedness, the same need.

The collapse of the Italian forces in September 1943, the German occupation and the partisan struggle brought others to her door for help, calling for redoubled secrecy. Besides resistance fighters there were the victims of persecution, fleeing prisoners of war and families bombed out of their homes – a hoard of fugitives all with different needs.

Naturally, a number of scoundrels managed to find their way among those in genuine need, but the Daughters were instructed to give to everyone without asking too many questions. They knew from St Paul that charity "bears all things, believes all things, hopes all things, endures all things" (1 Cor 13:7).

In October 1943 the Anglo-American forces landed in southern Italy and began to fight their way up the peninsula against fierce opposition from the Germans. It was becoming clear that the war would roll over the whole length of Italy from south to north like a stone-crusher.

During that same month on the heights of Montecassino Abbot Diamare had a premonition. He suggested that the Benedictine nuns would be wise to move from their monastery and leave the monks to stay on alone in the ancient abbey. Not knowing where to go, the sisters set off for Rome, arriving one evening at the Abbey of St Paul Outside the Walls. Unfortunately there was no room, but someone thought of the Daughters of St Paul; could they perhaps accommodate some of the party in their Generalate? There were 28 of them, including the abbess, who was a paralytic. Thecla had no hesitation: "Let them all come!" she said.

They were to stay for almost a year. Immediately on arrival they were taken to the refectory for a meal, where they quite failed to recognise the Prima Maestra among the others as she helped to carry dirty dishes into the kitchen. As well as food they were given winter clothing, and Thecla checked that every one of the nuns had a woollen vest rather than a cotton one. She tried to make them feel as far as possible as though they were in their own home, following the rhythms of cloister, observing the Hours according to their custom. She even asked the Daughters to entertain them with poetry recitals. "The Benedictines need to be cheered up; let's try to make them forget they're far from home." It was her unhappy duty, in February 1944, to break the appalling news to the sisters that they no longer had a home to return to, that Montecassino had been bombed to rubble.

In August 1944, three months after the liberation of Rome, the allied administration assigned a villa on the Via Laurentina to the Benedictine sisters. The Daughters of St Paul turned this move into a kind of celebration, helping them to carry their provisions, kitchen equipment, furniture and sacred objects. One of the nuns recalls that several years later, when they were finally able to return to Montecassino, Thecla "arranged for the mother abbess to travel in her own car. The help we received from the Daughters was absolutely crucial; indeed for the journey back to Cassino we needed 16 lorries to carry all the things we had acquired."

Above all they returned with new strength, due in no small measure to their contact with someone whose mere presence was itself a reassurance. Many nuns still remember how the Prima Maestra would walk calmly up and down during the long hours in the air raid shelter. Sister Giuseppina Balestra, who drove her car, recalls: "I so much admired her strength during the war. We watched her praying as she walked among us in the shelter where we spent countless hours. It was as though she was reviewing her troops; the very sight of her gave us courage. She would often say, 'Let's take all the precautions we can, trust in God and then put our minds at rest. The Primo Maestro says that nothing will happen to us.'"

"The Primo Maestro says..." For her the words of Fr Alberione were nothing less than a manifestation of the will of God, though from time to time it was accompanied by thunder and lightening. She was occasionally seen "red in the face as she ran into chapel", a scene witnessed by the Benedictine sisters. They also heard her speaking quietly to herself: "Help me to pray, so that I may obey cheerfully..."

She desperately wanted to obey, but from time to time her strong self-will resisted with equal desperation.

Then there were her responsibilities as Prima Maestra. She held that position as the gift of Fr Alberione and knew very well that it was he she had to answer to. But she felt equally and strongly her responsibilities to God and the Daughters of St Paul, women who at a sign from her could find themselves setting out for the other end of the world, taking their chance with peace and war, good health and ill. It was all very distressing and hurtful.

Her continued ill health did not help matters. The anxieties and physical trials of the war years left her in poor health, and in the summer of 1945 she moved back to Alba for a time in the hope of regaining her strength.

Alberione wrote to her in August: "Dear Prima Maestra, they tell me that you're already a little better. I thank God for the benefit that the Daughters will derive from this, especially here in Rome." He then goes on to speak of the extensions needed to the house at Grottaferrata, of the physical exhaustion of the sisters in many other houses ("several of them need at least a year of convalescence after all they've been through!") and lastly about the great church to be built in Rome in honour of Mary Queen of Apostles.

She was poorly again in November. "For some time now I have been letting others reply to your letters;" she wrote in one of her circulars, "I simply can't do everything because of my health." She dutifully obeyed her doctor's orders to rest a little each morning and afternoon. She was anxious to rebuild her strength before the end of the year because she wanted to make another journey. It would be her first since the war, and Fr Alberione was to accompany her.

It was the first journey for both of them as heads of recognised institutes of the Universal Church. On 10 May 1941 Pius XII had signed the *decretum laudis* which conferred the first pontifical recognition on the Pious Society of St Paul, granting provisional approval to their Constitutions for seven years.

Then on 13 December 1943, after so many years of waiting, the Pious Society of the Daughters of St Paul was raised to the same dignity, a great step forward in which Bishop Grassi had also played a part.

By air from one America to the other

It would be a great joy to see the American Daughters after so many years. They had been extremely generous to the Mother house with their help during the war, sending money, clothes and food. Correspondence was difficult for much of this time: there were long delays and letters went astray. Often the only means of contact was indirect: "I'm writing to you so that you can let so-and-so know..."

We get some idea of the problems from the Prima Maestra's letters to the Daughters in Latin America. This was not simply a news bulletin but an attempt to continue the routine management of those distant communities, fulfilling all the requirements of the Constitutions just as in peace time – religious professions and admissions to the noviciate to be recorded. Some extracts from letters to Maestra Brigida convey the flavour of this correspondence:

January 1942: "I do hope you've received my latest letters by now. I've written twice since the date of your last one. I'm happy with the arrangements for the professions and the noviciate. We have the details of the five to be admitted. They will have entered by now. The sisters at Florida [Argentina] have been asking me for some time for a copy of the Constitutions to give to the bishop. We can't send them from here. Don't you have a copy? I'm so glad to hear that you're printing *Familia Cristiana*. Here *Famiglia Cristiana* has reached 80,000 copies..."

August 1942: "This is a very difficult situation – not being able to communicate quickly with each other. May God's will be done! It's nearly a year since we had any word from Brazil. Please write asking them to send something through you..."

November 1945, when the war was over: "They tell me that you've been very ill. How are you now? Don't worry

143

about sending help; Maestra Paula has come to the rescue. We were very short of clothing but now we have enough for everyone. It isn't worth the expense of sending anything. São Paulo has sent us two parcels of stuff, but they have been held up for nearly two months at Naples and there seems no hope of getting them out. If you can't send things with someone coming over it's better not to bother. Meanwhile you can start asking for charity offerings for Italy. We have so many people that need help. What a sorry mess our poor country is in! It drives you to tears!"

At last they were able to travel. On 12 December 1945 Fr Alberione and four of his priests, along with Maestra Thecla and a group of sisters, boarded the liner *Andrea Gritti* bound for New York, where they arrived on 11 January 1946. The party included Fr Borrano, who was returning to the States, and Maestra Paula Cordero. The Founder and the Prima Maestra then continued on their travels: sometimes together, sometimes separately, according to circumstances. Between 9 February and 4 April they were in Brazil and Argentina, a journey which gave Thecla her first taste of air travel. She returned via New York, sailing on the *Vulcania* and arriving at Naples on 22 May 1946.

"This must be a year of progress for all of us. I hope that when I return I shall find you all better disposed and holier." So she wrote to the Daughters on the outward journey. There was now so much more to do in the world than before. But before they could *do* something, the apostles had to *be* something. All the rest – production, distribution methods, questions of management – was absolutely secondary.

Back in the United States Thecla succumbed once again to the spell of that great country with its multitude of peoples and cultures. For her it would always be the most compelling challenge to the Pauline apostolate in the western world. It was also the most persuasive demonstration that Fr Alberione had been inspired and guided to send his missionaries there at the right moment. As she wrote towards the end of January 1946: "The more I travel, the more I realise the enormous task of our apostolate. We really must thank the Lord every day for having called us to form a Congregation which is so appropriate to the times, for being allowed to feel a justifiable pride." On 25 January, the feast of the Conversion of St Paul, she shared a joyful discovery with the sisters in Italy: "What pleased me more than anything was to see how much the Daughters here love St Paul: even more than we do!" These were the sisters who travelled on the Staten Island ferry with their bags of books. When war broke out between Italy and the United States in December 1941 they found that communications with home were immediately suspended. From that same moment they found themselves confronted with the new mission of ministering to Italian prisoners of war.

It was a pleasant surprise for the thousands of them who arrived on the other side of the Atlantic to discover these Italian nuns. It was like finding something of home, much as Thecla herself was offering hospitality in Rome to individuals, families and communities – sometimes for only an hour or so, but often for months at a time. It was part of her charisma: to make everyone feel at home, to "invite the hungry to sit down on the grass". The Italian prisoners in America were certainly not starving; it was home and Italy that they missed, and the Daughters of St Paul were glad to be able to recreate something of that atmosphere for them. They made sure that priests were available for the celebration of Sunday Mass; they organised visits by relatives who lived in the United States, including the father of one of the prisoners; and they encouraged reading by distributing tens of thousands of religious books. Thecla could be justifiably proud of these sisters, whose work was so firmly rooted in the spirit of St Paul. And for the benefit of the other Daughters back home she wrote: "We in Italy ought really to feel a little humble for not having brought more people to a devotion to St Paul."

She then flew on with Fr Alberione to Brazil, where she

stayed at São Paulo and met both the community of that city and the sisters from Porto Alegre. Here she had the happiness of seeing again all those pioneers who had been coming over since 1932. They had survived the long years of isolation, though many of them had experienced moments of crisis during the war, when Thecla's precarious transatlantic correspondence had sustained and guided them through their many problems.

Somehow she had continued to hold them by the hand, as it were, through the years when things were difficult. Now the Brazilian Daughters could show her the premises they had constructed on their own plot of land, the new printing shop, the plans for the four-storey building which was to be erected in 1947.

Then there were the new faces, the essentially Brazilian contribution to the spread of the word of God: "They have 15 adult postulants and the same number of young girls," she announced in one of her circulars. This noviciate was founded in 1940, and over the next few years several Brazilian Daughters would leave for Rome to carry on their studies in theology – the first of them, in fact, returned with Thecla to Italy.

This visit to the front line inspired a number of letters which at times become hymns of thanksgiving for what the Daughters had managed to achieve, for what was promised by the new arrivals – so young, so full of life, so open and straightforward in their spontaneity. "Whichever region I visit and whoever I speak to, I always come to understand better that we, the Daughters of St Paul, are the Lord's favoured ones: firstly because of the great grace of the religious vocation which has been granted to us, and secondly because he has sent us to work in this holy apostolate of the press."

In Argentina she found another noviciate in full operation, canonically instituted in 1940, whilst another large formation house was still being erected. The sisters had also created two branch houses. One of these, at Rosario, was opened as early as 1936, where the local bishop, Mgr Antonio Caggiano, a future Cardinal Archbishop of Buenos Aires, was a great support. Indeed he was the originator of an idea which enabled them to become known very quickly: he suggested that they should follow him round the diocese on his pastoral visits. The other branch house was opened in the suburbs of Santa Fé in 1940, in premises which soon proved too small. It was transferred to the centre of the city in 1950.

On her return from this journey she seemed to be physically renewed. The Daughters had now reached the moment for expansion on all fronts. "Our apostolate needs wider development and consequently a larger number of sisters." She dictated a long circular on this subject which contained the most minute instructions about the work to be done for vocations and the criteria of selection. This special apostolate called for a very special kind of postulant. "Do not let yourselves believe that by choosing with greater care you will find fewer candidates. By accepting only the most suitable young women you ensure an enduring advantage to the Congregation, for this increases its reputation and in turn it serves to attract more postulants of similar calibre."

She again omitted to mention this journey to her family before leaving; her convalescence at Alba in the summer of 1945 had reminded her mother about her ailing health and she did not wish to give further cause for concern. Now she was able to put the old lady's mind at rest: "I have just completed another journey to America and I am very well; in fact, far from tiring me out, the trip has done me good. And how are you? Did you manage to get out to cast your vote?" Sunday 2 June 1946 was the date of elections to the Constituent Assembly and of the referendum to chose between the monarchy and a republic. In Rome all the Daughters had gone to vote and, with Thecla at their head, they had queued for a long time outside the polling booths.

She wrote again to her mother in December 1946,

combining Christmas greetings with seasonal advice: "Now that it's winter, be sure you keep warm and look after yourself. I pray for you always, dear mother, and I remember you every day." This was probably her last letter to her mother, who died at the age of eighty only a few weeks later on 18 January 1947.

A prayer for Palmiro Togliatti

One day in October 1918 a young child of nine who had just lost her mother was walking, hand in hand with her father, through the streets of Susa. The father wanted to place her in the care of that group of girls who were printing the diocesan newspaper, believing that they ran some kind of school. On meeting the twenty-eight-year-old Teresa Merlo he was dismayed to find that this was not a place for girls of such tender years. On the other hand, Teresa herself was equally appalled at the idea of abandoning that child to an unknown future, and in the end she decided to accept her, taking on the roles of mother, sister and teacher.

That child of nine, Maestra Irene Conti, could not have known as she walked along the streets of Susa that she was setting out on a much longer journey – to Japan, in fact, wearing the habit of the Daughters of St Paul, and sent there by that same Teresa who had taken her by the hand on that far-away October day.

In the spring of 1947, Maestra Conti and her companions Palmira Bernardini and Lorenzina Nota, Vicenza Prestofilippo were received in audience by Pope Pius XII before their departure. "Your Holiness," she said, "we are about to leave for Japan, but we don't know the language, or anything..." Pius XII smiled as he gave them several blessings for the various needs of their journey. Above all, he emphasised the importance of the interior life, and they seemed to hear again the words of Maestra Thecla, who may not have been Pope, yet said precisely the same things, preached the same growth of the spirit, and taught them *to be* rather than merely *to do.*

The American houses had already been reinforced as far as means would allow, but Fr Alberione had not forgotten the Far East. Fr Paolo Marcellino, on leave at the Mother house in Rome after 12 years in the Orient, had formed a great love for that part of the world – an infectious enthusiasm which he imparted to all who heard him speak of his experiences.

However, getting to Japan was a complicated business in those days. The four Daughters found themselves following Columbus, approaching the East by way of the West. They travelled from Italy to New York, where they stayed nine months; then in January 1948 they crossed the United States to California and from there embarked for the Philippines. They finally landed on 6 August 1948 at Yokohama, and Fr Paolo Marcellino was there to greet them and take them to an apartment in Tokyo which he had prepared. Two young Japanese girls were on hand to teach them how to get about the city, and how to live and work in this very different style of accommodation.

They were observing one of Maestra Thecla's oldest precepts – learning joyfully about the customs of another people, learning to appreciate their traditions, to understand their culture, as the Apostle Paul had done for the whole of his missionary life. Maestra Irene recalls those early days in Japan: "There was great poverty, and it was impossible to obtain many of the necessities of life. The first vocations came from among the poor, but Maestra Thecla encouraged us to accept them and to give them what they needed. 'Poverty', she said, 'should not be an obstacle to the acceptance of a vocation.'"

Meanwhile the Prima Maestra made a tour of the Daughters' houses throughout Italy, paying particular attention to the fostering of vocations. During this period she and the Founder spoke in continuous unison about the need for new recruits. Now that the Pauline family had received full ecclesiastical approval it urgently needed to increase its numbers. It was essential to catch the tide of this post-war period of psychological revival. Certainly, vocations were at the Lord's disposal; but the sisters had to be ready to collaborate with him by inviting possible candidates to consider the religious life, by drawing attention to the work of the Congregation and by providing information about themselves. The Daughters had to make the first move. Sister Giuseppina Balestra was her driver during this time and she recalls: "During our journeys, whilst we were crossing great tracts of countryside dotted with hamlets and isolated farmhouses, she would often ask herself, 'I wonder if the Daughters of St Paul have passed this way, bringing the word of God to these people? Let's pray that they have!' And then we would immediately say a short prayer for the people and for vocations."

It was on just such a journey, as they were travelling from one house to another that Maestra Thecla's car was brought to a halt at a road-block at San Donà di Piave in the Veneto region. It was impossible to continue; there were serious disorders following news from Rome that Palmiro Togliatti, head of the Italian Communist Party, had been shot and seriously wounded. A general strike had been called and people were already talking about revolution. "The Prima Maestra was deeply upset by this painful news, but she thanked God that the injury had not been mortal. We turned back as far as Treviso and for the whole of that journey she prayed both for Togliatti and for those responsible for the attack."

News of new conquests arrived back at the General house throughout the year in 1948. Four nuns left for Colombia in April: Maestra Letizia Ellena and her companions Elisea Vaschetto, Imelda Toschi and Luigina Grandi. They had to spend the night of their arrival at the port of Cartagena before catching a plane for Bogota, where they were welcomed by the men of the Society. After a few weeks they opened their first house, which naturally enough was the usual "Bethlehem", with the customary defects – too little space and an inconvenient position. In addition, Bogota stands at more than 8,000 feet above sea level and, like all new arrivals, the sisters had problems of acclimatisation.

In May there was another new establishment, at Valparaiso in Chile, founded by Maestra Giulia Toschi and Sister Fulgida Sandrini. Two more sisters were later sent to reinforce this mission.

At the same time a start was being made in Mexico by Maestra Bernadetta Ferraris, accompanied by Diomira Trolli, Thecla Ziliante and Annunciata Spada. In the capital, Mexico City, the sisters were bound by law to wear normal dress. Their first task was to visit homes and to distribute the books printed by the men of the Society, who had been working there for some years. The effort to promote Mexican vocations was soon rewarded, for three novices were already studying in Rome by 1950.

Maestra Thecla's tour of the Italian houses finished in September 1948 and one of her short circulars of that time speaks of "so much goodwill and such a desire to do good". She had found that there was great mutual help between individual sisters and between one house and another. Her December circular was unusually long and concentrated that year, urging the Daughters on to further expansion, but emphasising the need to improve the quality of their recruitment as well as increasing numbers. She recalls Article 124 of the Constitutions as drawn up at that time, which states that "the practice of poverty is the foundation and treasure of the religious life and of the apostolate".

She explains that perfection requires day-by-day attention, so that a Daughter may become always more worthy to be a bearer of the Word. She explains the importance of imitating the poverty of Jesus from the cradle to the grave, studying at the feet of the saints and their most successful imitators. "The saints chose for their own use the poorest and simplest objects; let us try to cultivate the same 'refined tastes'." This spiritual elegance is purest Thecla: poverty seen as an enrichment, as something which enhances the dignity of the person, as she makes clear in a later passage: "Don't let us have unreasonable expectations. It would surely be a disgrace if we did not know how to do without things that perhaps we might never have enjoyed if we had remained in the world."

By the nature of their calling, the Daughters of St Paul have always had to deal with money and material things, and on a scale never dreamed of in the earliest religious families. The Constitutions address this matter and laid down rules of conduct, which were taken up by Maestra Thecla in this circular: "Be careful to obtain the necessary permissions when it comes to 'giving or receiving', even if it is only a small matter. In particular, those who routinely handle money should always exercise the greatest care." They must be "scrupulous in their book-keeping" and "exercise economy in their purchases", though without falling into the opposite defect. "But poverty is clearly not meanness; nor is it untidiness, lack of decorum, of propriety or of cleanliness."

Some of her circulars, taken together, make up a kind of course of instruction, complete with revision material. Meanwhile, the Daughters' establishments were multiplying across the world, and their number increased with a rush of new recruits. By now all generations were represented in the Congregation: it had its older members as well as its young; those near to the Mother house and those on the other side of the world. All of these had to be formed and guided towards a common spirit of evangelisation. Theirs was a difficult task, which did not always become easier with the years, for a Daughter lives almost continually in the public eye, and her conduct is constantly under scrutiny– her way of speaking, of offering a book, of dealing with other sisters, of entering a home. Even her telephone manner or her style at the wheel of a car are liable to be noted as a reflection of the Congregation.

It is a difficult vocation, unprotected by convent walls, or even a door. In the long run it becomes a burden. Thecla knew this well and, in a circular of March 1949, she returned to the subject of motivation. It was natural enough that women who were constantly on the move, knocking on doors to sell books, should from time to time experience a crisis of will. If the sole purpose was to achieve sales, could they really be expected to carry on relentlessly in the face of fatigue, lack of creature comforts, and all manner of receptions at the hands of the public? If that really were the only objective, boredom and discontent would inevitably follow. The only ones to stay the course would be those who saw the task as a way of reaching out to people for their spiritual good. This is neither more nor less than a continuation of the work of the apostles, who left, two by two, at Our Lord's command: "The Daughters of St Paul must continue this apostolate – always in twos, always in manner, light and pure as the doves which fly over the mud bringing the olive-branch to all, the word of peace, the example of modesty, humility and commitment."

Maestra Thecla was now to travel the world repeating these things, across the mountains and beyond the oceans. On 3 April 1949 she left with Fr Alberione to visit the Pauline establishments in India, the Philippines, Japan, Mexico and the United States. It was to be a journey of four months and she would circle the globe.

Thecla entranced by the East

By the beginning of 1949, the civil war in China was rapidly drawing to an end with victory for the communist army of Mao Tse-tung. In January, having defeated the nationalist troops of Chiang Kai-shek, the "reds" occupied Peking, the seat of residence of the imperial family for centuries, and Mao Tse-tung wrote a poem commemorating his return to the capital after 31 years. Chiang had his capital at Nanking; but his nationalists were unable to defend it and Mao's armada captured it on 24 April.

These events forced Fr Alberione to miss a visit which he had been looking forward to with particular eagerness. The Pauline house at Nanking had been re-established in 1938 by Fr Giuseppe Pio Bertino and Fr Ercole Clemente Canavero, who had returned to their posts during a lull in the Sino-Japanese war. As he later wrote: "The so-called Iron Curtain had moved unexpectedly. Travel to Nanking was impossible and there was no means of contacting our people, even by telephone or radio. I tried to bring forward my departure from Rome so as to arrive before they were cut off. It was with enormous sorrow that I had to content myself with sending them my blessing as I flew over the China Sea and the nearby regions."

The journey of the Founder and Maestra Thecla began on 3 April 1949, when they left [Rome's] Ciampino airport for Delhi. At the Indian capital he had a most beautiful meeting which he recorded in his diary in these words: "Had the great consolation of seeing Fr Alfonso Ferrero and Brother Bernardino (Ruffoli) again after 12 years. Both show the after-effects of illness and of more than six years behind barbed wire. They are absolutely authentic followers of St Paul."

The two travellers separated here. Fr Alberione stayed on, whilst Maestra Thecla proceeded to Calcutta and the Philippines. As she moved from one place to the next the sea of eastern humanity made a deep impression on her, causing pangs of love and pain. Her heart went out to those thousands of poor, half-naked people moving about like so many ants through the buildings and streets of Calcutta. Faced with such poverty she felt that she owed them at least a word; that she must break the silence; do something to communicate. But she knew no phrase that would convey her feelings, and of her own tongue they would have understood nothing.

She was particularly struck by the servant girls who "are considered inferior and keep their distance". She noticed one with pendants on her nose and rings on her feet. They looked at each other, and the Indian woman, recognising Thecla as a nun, made the sign of the cross. "This morning she asked me for a picture of Jesus, so I gave her a small blessed crucifix. She was quite delighted." India had become independent in 1947 and, at the time of her visit, was passing through a most difficult period of adjustment. Gandhi had been assassinated, and the process of evolving a democratic constitution was attended by civil conflict and much misery.

No nun was ever happier to arrive in the Philippines. Approaching Manila she must have thought back to those letters that she sent during the war, speaking of misfortunes without end: "You have lost everything, but at least you yourselves are safe and sound!" And again: "What are you doing now that you lost all your machinery for the printing apostolate? And have the fathers also lost everything? Let's hope that you can soon get the presses working again and start doing some good again among all those poor people... In Italy too almost everything has been destroyed: railways, bridges, whole towns. Let us try to be holy and to console the Lord."

At last she arrived at Manila to find, waiting on the tarmac to greet her, the Daughters who had survived the invasion of China, the invasion of the Philippines and the mass migrations under bombardment. They had an infinity of things to say to each other, a true feast to celebrate, and yet they walked in silence. Sister Cleofe Zanoni, one of the survivors, recalls: "There we were, all dressed in white, and she, in the middle of us, in black. The faces of all of us were streaming with perspiration and with tears, and she tried to console us: 'I'll be with you for more than a month; there will be time enough for us to exchange all our news.'"

The Daughters did not have a car and they wanted to hire one for her. But she refused: "Ordinary people don't travel like that here, so why should I?" So public transport it was, with no fuss; she would travel as everyone else did. She encouraged them to talk about their experiences, and she listened to everything – including things that some of them at first did not dare speak of – just like a real family. They had lost everything, but they had now begun all over again. They were selling a lot of books and they already felt the need to make a start with films. Thecla had been thinking along similar lines during the journey, for there were cinemas everywhere, with bright façades and enormous posters advertising their programmes. She almost shouted with joy when she first saw the countryside of the Philippines: "What marvels of nature you enjoy here and what a beautiful sky you have! I feel we're nearer to heaven."

The eyes of the young Philippine postulants shone brightly. These new recruits were ready for action both in their own country and far overseas, for as the Prima Maestra used to say, "The world is large... wherever you land you find different people," and Jesus Christ had to be proclaimed to all of them. So during the whole period of forty days that she spent with them, as they exchanged their news, as they relaxed during the hour of recreation, even as they darned their stockings, she conducted a course of revision and up-dating of their missionary spirituality. The Prima Maestra spoke, as she invariably did, about "the good of souls", an expression typical of those times, which we today may consider dated, preferring the language of psychology or avoiding the concept altogether. For her, however, the soul was everything. That immortal spark in all of us was the basis of universal brotherhood, binding together millions and indeed billions of human beings on this earth. It was by starting with "the good of souls" – as she had learned from Fr Pistone at Castagnito, from Canon Chiesa at Alba and from the Primo Maestro himself – that Thecla succeeded in breaking down all barriers, external and internal. For example, the sisters at Lipa wanted to make a Sunday visit to some distant townships where the people lived in particularly wretched conditions and had no priest; but they were distressed at the idea of having to go without

Mass and Communion. Thecla herself had no hesitation: anything could be sacrificed to comfort those poor people with a visit, a word of consolation. Christ had to be brought to people wherever they were, whatever their condition.

Fr Alberione eventually joined her and together they travelled to Tokyo. Here, the sisters who had told Pius XII that they did not know the language were making good progress with it. They had already started a Sunday catechism school and were receiving their first Japanese postulants. The American occupation was now at an end. United States' policy, which had at first favoured the dismantling of Japanese industry, was beginning to change, following the communist victory in China. The country which had been defeated in 1945 was now becoming necessary to a defensive system designed to ensure peace and security in the Far East. Gradually, the conditions were being created for the emergence of Japan over the next few decades as an economic super-power.

The activities of the Society of St Paul in Tokyo aimed at reflecting both the great Japanese national cultural tradition and the unprecedented situation left in the wake of the war. It was a Pauline initiative which brought into being a Japanese cultural radio station, in which the Daughters also played their part. The young Japanese postulants were amazed and delighted to note how the Prima Maestra set about patching and sewing the sisters' personal linen.

She in turn quickly came to like these people: "It seemed such a difficult thing to attempt to evangelise the Japanese; but the Primo Maestro told them to make a start, and now the Daughters are working just as they do in Italy and in other countries. They are well received everywhere and by everyone, both Protestants and pagans." (She used the word "pagan" as interchangeable with "non-Christian".)

From Japan she proceeded to Mexico City, where she arrived on 6 June. The Daughters had been here barely a year, and Thecla was amazed at the results they had already achieved, in particular the enormous number of books they had managed to distribute. The people too were very fond of the sisters and were delighted with the work they were doing. But, as always, there were still too few of them. "They are trying very hard to find recruits here, as well as in Japan and the Philippines, but what they really want is professed sisters from Italy. Will they be able to spare any?"

Having arrived back home via the United States and Portugal, she summarised her conclusions from the journey in a circular of 24 July. Listing "a few of the things learned", she returned again to Fr Alberione's idea: "I have come to understand that of ourselves we are nothing, that we count for nothing, and that we can achieve nothing without God's grace. We must therefore always remain humble and pray for God's help. Without it we only know how to spoil things; but the Lord achieves great things when he finds souls that are submissive and humble."

Then there came her unfailing reminder about vocations: "Out there I see so many souls waiting to be saved, yet so few labourers working on behalf of the Gospel. Just think! There is still one half of the human race that does not know God, whilst the other half knows him, but heeds him little or not at all. In every house I listen to complaints about the shortage of sisters, to pleas for help. Some Daughters speak enthusiastically about the missions and beg to be allowed to go; but then, woe betide anyone who tries to shift them from the little nest they have built for themselves! What we need is a heart that is truly missionary, generous, detached from worldly comforts and ready to answer any call."

It was on 27 June 1949, whilst Alberione and Thecla were away on this journey, that Pius XII conceded full and final recognition to the Pious Society of St Paul when he granted definitive approval to the Institute and its Constitutions. Article 2 states that the purpose of the Society consists in "propagating Catholic doctrine, particularly by the apostolate of communications – that is through the press, motion pictures, radio and television – as well as by other more effective and expeditious media or inventions of the age which human progress may make available and the necessities and conditions of the times may require."

It is appropriate to anticipate here another historic event, namely the definitive pontifical recognition of the Pious Society of the Daughters of St Paul. This took place on 15 March 1953, and the Constitutions which were approved included the following words about the purpose of the women's Congregation: "That the religious work with all their energies for the glory of God and the salvation of souls in the spreading of Catholic doctrine with the apostolate of the editions: press, cinema, radio, television, and in general with ther most expeditious and fruitful means; that is, the inventions which human progress furnishes and the necessities and the conditions of the times require."

Though they date from the reign of Pius XII, these texts have a flavour which anticipates *Inter mirifica*, the second Vatican Council's Decree on the means of social communications of December 1963.

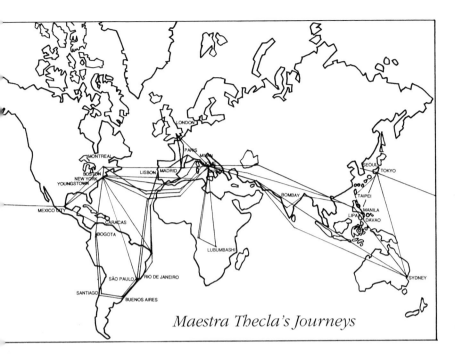

Maestra Thecla's Journeys

Maestra Thecla's Journeys embraced five continents.

Right: *On her first visit to Kinshasa (Zaire) in November 1961. The Daughters began work there in 1958.*

Kinshasa 1961: Thecla smiles amid a throng of young boys fascinated by the camera.

Right: *Cebu (Philippines) 1962: Thecla is welcomed at the airport with the traditional garland of flowers.*

Bombay 1962: With a group of young postulants and their relatives, celebrating their first steps in religious life.

India 1960: The camera catches Thecla in a moment of leisure during her visit to the Bombay community.

Right: *A young Japanese girl presents Thecla with a bouquet.*

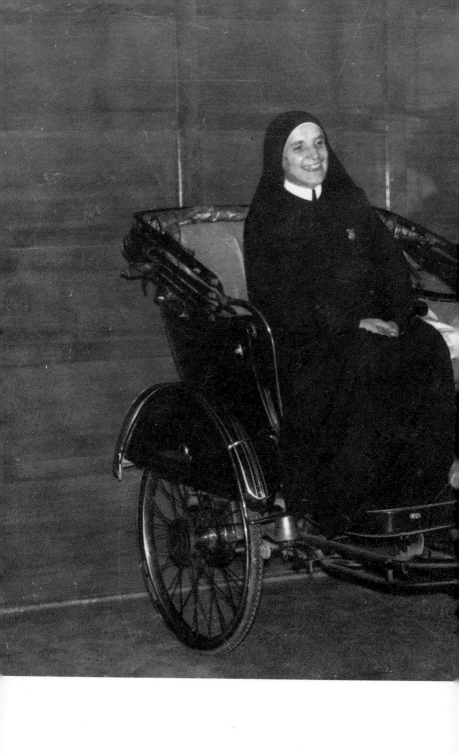

Taipei (Taiwan) 1962: The Superior General was always ready to enjoy the lighter moments.

*1959: With the community at
Manizales (Colombia).*

Opposite, above: *Thecla alights
in the rain at the airport of Lins
(Brazil) in 1960.*

Opposite, below: *Thecla examines
a collection of ornamental stones
with a group of Brazilian sisters,
probably in the course of the same
journey.*

Albano Laziale, Rome, 22 August 1963: Thecla introduces members of the community to Pope Paul VI during his visit to the Regina Apostolorum *clinic.*

Below: *September 1963: A moment of relaxation with Fr. Alberione. The building under construction in the background is the new hospital.*

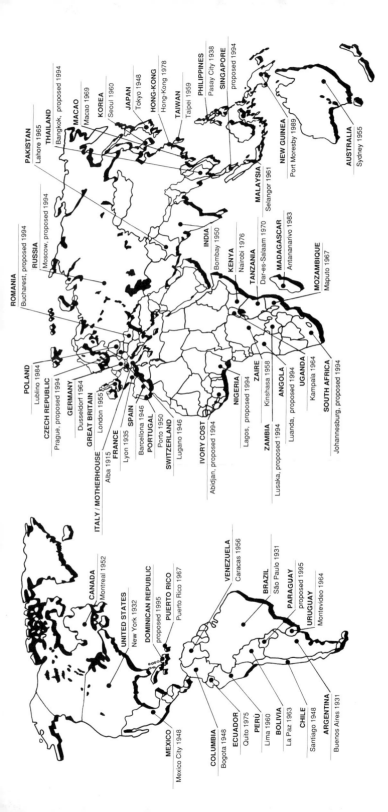

The communities of the Daughters of St Paul across the world in 1993, showing their locations and the dates of each foundation.

Albano Laziale, Rome, 1964: "We may not find joy in every moment of life but at least we can be at peace." Already seriously ill when this photograph was taken, Maestra Thecla maintained her serenity until her death on 5 February 1964.

Opposite: *The manuscript of 28 May 1961 in which Thecla offers her life for the sanctification of the Daughters of St Paul.*

Festa della S.S. Trinità.
Ariano 2? Maggio 1951

Offerta della mia vita
perché tutte le Figlie di
San Paolo si facciano
Sante.

Con cuore umiliato e con
tutto Vi prego Divine
Persone della S.S. Trinità
Padre, Figlio e Spirito
Santo, di accettare la
offerta della mia vita
per tutta la beatifi-
gazione delle Figlie di
San Paolo, che tutte si
facciano sante.
Tutto è vostro, anche
questa misera vita
ma che tutto si veda
da la maggior vostra
gloria o Trinità S.S.
e per compiere la S.S.
Vostra Volontà.
Tutto metto nelle
mani della S.S. Vergine
che pure lei o Maria
fai parte della Trinità
S.S. come Madre del
Figlio e Sposa dello
Spirito Santo
San Paolo dà a tutte
il suo amore a Dio
e zelo per le anime.
Così sia, ora e sempre
Suor Carla Maria

Ciampino Airport (Rome) 1956: Thecla embraces Maestra Ignazia, her eventual successor as Superior General, after a visit to the communities in the United States.

Chapter Six

WITH PROPHETIC CHARACTER
AND COURAGE

During a course of spiritual exercises in September 1949, Fr Alberione gave this counsel to the Daughters of St Paul: "Be simple... and take good care of the briskness and energy you were born with." Maestra Thecla enlarged on this idea in a circular of March 1950 and went into details, emphasising that "simplicity is a characteristic of our Institute: we must guard and protect it, resisting and doing our best to eliminate everything that tends to make us pompous and petty." She then translated this advice into ten practical points, which were to become famous in the Congregation as the "Decalogue of Briskness". Here they are:

1   Be brisk in dealings with the superiors and other sisters.
2   Be brisk on the telephone and in the parlour. Your speech should always be brief and edifying.
3   Be brisk and brief in your letters. Long letters are as bad as long speeches.
4   Be brisk in carrying out the orders you receive.
5   Be brisk in moving from one house to another, without regrets or sadness.
6   Be brisk in your greetings, on arrival or departure.
7   Be brisk in the Book and Film centres.
8   Be brisk in all the work you do.
9   Be brisk in your deportment, observing a proper religious dignity, but avoiding affectation.
10 Be brisk in the confessional: no long explanations – just clear and simple statements of the essentials and nothing more.

Points five and six concern transfers from one house to another, which sometimes upset those concerned or gave rise to over-elaborate farewells. These were all small matters, yet they all tended to harm the missionary spirit, and so in her eyes they were not acceptable.

Her continuous attention to details reflected her basic common sense. No one – and particularly a woman who had consecrated her life to God – could afford to ignore faults, even those that might seem trivial. Faults such as these, when tolerated and allowed to take root, worked against the authentic spirit of the Institute and were therefore a danger to all its members. We see here an echo of that rich peasant wisdom, found in country places all over the world, which defends the family's modest economy by questioning even the tiniest expense and guarding against all waste, from the spilled handful of grain to the lost coin. "Watch the small expenses! They don't make the same splash as the big ones, but together can do as much damage." Maestra Thecla observed the same care in managing the spiritual fortune of the Institute, in particular the riches she derived from her journeys.

The secret Thecla

Thecla had by now become her own teacher, albeit along lines laid down by Fr Alberione, and was constantly concerned to correct herself, measuring her behaviour against standards she had learned through her reading and from personal counsel, judging her faith on the evidence of her acts and omissions. This was the secret Thecla, who gave no quarter when she examined and analysed her actions. Nor did she make any allowances for herself in her spiritual notebooks, where we can read summaries of her retreats and spiritual exercises, complete with personal "balance sheets" and resolutions for the immediate future.

The year 1950 was proclaimed a Holy Year by Pope Pius XII and Maestra Thecla noted: "Let this Holy Year be one of special graces for me and for the Congregation. Let everything be in total accord with the Lord's will: everything under the maternal gaze of Our Blessed Lady." Her notes go on to outline a programme: "Holy Year 1950/51. I have started this year. Shall I finish it? I don't know. I want every minute, hour, day and month of this year to belong wholly and exclusively to God. I surrender my own will so that I may only do his. I give up my preferences, my opinions, so that I may only listen to God's. Let my whole life be a continuous *Magnificat* to God for so many graces received; let it be one long act of adoration."

At the end of 1950 Thecla finds fault with herself: "A rather stormy year in every sense: I have been uncharitable, impatient, untrusting, bad-tempered. A Holy Year, yes: but I have had little benefit from it. I trust in God's grace to let me celebrate at least one jubilee. I don't think good will has been wanting, but there has been so much weakness and failure to correspond with God's grace... My Jesus, mercy!"

She was already commenting unfavourably on herself during a retreat at the end of February 1951: "No progress." And she goes on to specify: "I have been hard and uncharitable; I have seen everything around me as ugly because I was ugly inside myself, full of pride, envy and ill-will. I mean to improve with the help of God and Our Blessed Lady. I do so want to show understanding to the sisters, to be a mother to them."

Then after the spiritual exercises of March 1951: "We mustn't live this vocation of ours in terror and anguish, but in love and with confidence in our heavenly Father. Let us do what we have to do and trust in God. When the time comes for us to be judged, God's decision will ultimately depend on how we have lived our lives. We must never lose hope. As long as we have a breath of life in us we have the capacity to become holy. We have been made for heaven and we must fight to earn our place there."

Her reflections continue with a consideration of the idea of self-denial, of the continuous example of sacrifice given by Jesus throughout his earthly life and on the need for hard choices: "We must deny ourselves until it hurts, until it humiliates, even to the point of servitude. This is the tragic but inevitable choice if we want to become holy. We must follow self-denial to the point where it becomes self-annihilation. We must re-dedicate ourselves to it every day, and the more we grow in holiness the better we shall understand its importance. Self-denial gives life all its beauty and its value.

"At the beginning it is easy. What is truly terrible is trying to maintain this resolution to the end of our days. It is a fearful daily burden. The great problem is to keep going right up to the *consummatum est*, beginning each day with an ever-greater awareness of our own weakness, and re-newing the resolution despite all the battles we have lost. Yet that is what constitutes the true beauty and glory of our life."

One day Fr Alberione spoke of her to the Pauline priest, Fr Domenico Spoletini: "You know, the Prima Maestra has given herself completely to God with total dedication. There isn't a fibre of her body that isn't governed by the spirit."

Yet the same Alberione, when he was in headlong pursuit of one of his private intuitions, or when he was simply in a hurry (which was nearly all the time), showed no special consideration for her as Prima Maestra. For all that he recognised in her a quite exceptional person, he was capable of treating her roughly. Worse still, his reprimands were sometimes administered in public, in front of her own sisters.

This, then, was the Thecla who springs from the pages of the spiritual notebooks. Rebukes of this kind drove her to tears, but then her self-control reasserted itself in surprising and sometimes heroic ways. The Founder's outbursts provoked no deep sighs, no "significant" glances: nothing but the most absolute silence. Thecla accepted these painful wounds, and her profound peace of soul even enabled her to thank Our Lord for the experience. Her thinking was that if the Primo Maestro spoke like that it was because "he had the duty and I the need."

This was self-sacrifice indeed, not merely an idea noted in a diary. It was knowing how to humble oneself; not just allowing oneself to be humiliated. As she noted after a retreat: "The Divine Master: 'Learn from me; for I am gentle and lowly in heart' (Mt 11:29). 'Whoever humbles himself will be exalted' (Mt 23:12) – not 'whoever is humbled'. Humility is truth: I am nothing; I am capable of nothing; I am worth nothing. I am a miserable sinner, the most miserable on the face of the earth. What do I expect? The humble person enjoys peace and tranquillity. She is content to trust in God. She sees the good in others and before everything else she sees the Lord in her brothers and sisters. Our Lord and Master is her example." Though the Founder bullied her to the point of tears, this never prevented her from recognising his true qualities and acknowledging what he stood for.

Her maternal foresight

They left together for the Americas on 21 March 1952 and were away until the middle of June, touching the United States, Canada (twice) and then Mexico, Colombia, Chile, Argentina and Brazil. They made a short stop in Portugal on their way home.

"It is a great pleasure to be able to report that in all the houses visited I have found enormous good will and a great keenness for good works. All instructions from Rome are accepted with pleasure and put into effect with love. There is enthusiasm for the apostolate everywhere and a great will to work." These are the customary words she uses in the circulars summarising the conclusions of her journeys. There are many other documents of the kind, and they evidence her joy at being able to bring to the attention of the rest of the Congregation, and the Pauline world at large, the efforts of the Daughters in the front line. This was one of the reasons why her visits to the more distant houses were invariably occasions for celebration. The sisters were grateful for the recognition of their patience and efficiency, so necessary to those who labour – often without apparent results – on stony ground. On many of these journeys the Founder and the Prima Maestra also visited together the houses of the Pauline fathers and brothers, where she was always most welcome – and not only because both men and women owed their ultimate allegiance to St Paul. The fact is that the men of the Society were greatly in her debt. These matters were not always known about, for no particular effort was made to noise them abroad. Perhaps even the Primo Maestro was not aware of all the details. Or perhaps he was. In any case they were well known to many of the sons of St Paul in Italy and throughout the world. The Mother General of the Pauline sisters also knew how to be a mother to priests and brothers.

Several of those she met on her travels round the world had once come to knock at her door. It had been Fr Alberione's way to dispatch them from one continent to another virtually without notice and with hands practically empty. Some of them called on the Prima Maestra, perhaps not quite knowing what to ask and with no clear idea about their needs and priorities. And they must have reminded her of her brothers at Castagnito, when her mother Vincenza put a coin or a handkerchief into their pockets, or when she made up parcels of vests and socks for them as they left for the war: an enlightened generosity with well-chosen and practical gifts, and all done "briskly" and without fuss.

So if certain young men, sent out on unplanned missions, managed to survive the first dark days and months of their adventure, it was due at least in part to her knowledge of the situation and to her generosity. These men were always glad to see her on her travels, and when they returned to Italy they would go immediately to call on her and to offer well-earned thanks. As often as not they came away with another gift.

She also gave generous practical help to individuals, often in the form of substantial financial help where the case was serious enough. Fr Silvano Gratilli tells of one such incident: "Older people will remember the tragic story of the fire in a warehouse which had been built on behalf of the parish of Jesus the Good Shepherd, near to the Generalate. Several persons were killed in the incident, and although no one was to blame, the responsibility was attributed to the priest who had built it and who managed it. The Prima Maestra's generosity came promptly to the aid of this man, who found himself under enormous pressure, and she sent him, among other things, a considerable sum of money. She said, "I have not yet spoken about it to the Council, but I am letting you have this straightaway because we must do anything to avoid a priest being ruined"'.

That was by no means the only incident of this kind. She dealt with many other cases of need, some of them serious. In fact priests came to her for many different reasons, from practical matters to spiritual difficulties and problems of obedience and community life. Men who were learned in Latin and who had studied theology still felt the need to listen to the considered opinions of this completely genuine person, knowing that they would be understood. Sometimes they found that they had been understood even before they opened their mouths – for she had a penetrating eye – and on all these things she kept her own silent counsel and prayed. People found her able to make everything so simple and they invariably left her refreshed.

Fr Renato Perino, the third successor of the Primo Maestro, has pointed out this quality of hers: "Many members of the Society are deeply in Maestra Thecla's debt for her timely and invaluable advice about their vocation and their mission. There were moments when her maternal foresight seemed to be guided by Divine Providence or by the hand of Our Lady. The same can be said of sisters belonging to other congregations and orders, who received invaluable advice from this elderly mother superior in times of difficulty, as well as a personal interest prompted by her truly maternal tenderness."

Returning from her journeys she often spoke of the use of the potential of the cinema for spreading God's Word; she had grasped its ability to speak to and to influence all types of people. From her practical point of view as a missionary she could easily visualise the usefulness of this medium as an aid to preaching the Gospel – even, in some cases, as a temporary substitute for the missionary herself, where they were few and over-worked.

Fr Alberione too had quickly recognised the cinema as one of "the most expeditious and fruitful means" of spreading the Gospel, and also as a means of civic and moral instruction. He had discussed the subject at length with Canon Chiesa at Alba in the Twenties, and Article 285 of the 1954 edition of the Constitutions of the Daughters of St Paul speaks clearly on the subject: "Since the cinema exercises a most extensive influence in promoting good as well as in insinuating evil, the Daughters of St Paul must use this means of a very effective apostolate for the salvation of souls and the good of civil society itself."

In 1936 Pius XI pronounced this typically forthright judgement on a film which he considered harmful to children and young persons: "We are inevitably reminded of Our Lord's terrible words of condemnation against those who corrupt the young when we hear of the dangers to the souls of young boys and girls, of the loss of innocence, which lie in wait within some of our cinemas."

During the Thirties the production company REF (*Romana Editrice Film*) was formed, its inauguration being marked by an hour of prayer at the tomb of the Apostle Paul in Rome. The name was subsequently changed to *Sampaolo Film*, its purpose being to make films which on their own merits could be shown in the ordinary cinemas. It was able to achieve this – despite many difficulties and considerable hostility – through the film *Abuna Messias*, dedicated to the Capuchin missionary, Guglielmo Massaja, the Apostle of the Galla tribe of Ethiopia. The Capuchins were among others who contributed to the enterprise and Maestr a Thecla also gave material help.

Operations were suspended until the end of the second World War, when there was a change of policy. Though a few films in the pre-war style were produced, the company began to make "shorts" and documentaries, most of them with a catechetical purpose, which were greatly enjoyed and were considered timely and useful.

Not long after the war Maestra Thecla happened to meet Fr Emilio Cordero, the manager of *Sampaolo Film*, who spoke of the opportunities and problems of the cinema as a medium for catechesis. Maestra Ignazia Balla, at that time one of her close associates, remembered the occasion: "She was greatly impressed by what she had heard and I remember her talking about it with enthusiasm. There was a great work for good to be done through the cinema; it was an apostolate in which the Daughters of St Paul should become actively involved. It would certainly be a difficult field, but it was both necessary and urgent to tackle it. Moreover, the Founder had said that they should begin to work in the cinema and this was enough to convince the Prima Maestra that it was the will of God. We had to do it, whatever the cost."

Here was another example of her ready obedience. She gave immediate instructions for the Daughters of St Paul, despite their heavy load of other duties, to start to concern themselves with the cinema. This was the beginning of the process which in the course of time produced those expert sisters who advised both priests and lay organisations about a new field in which they were completely without skills. This is how another Daughter of St Paul, Maestra Rosaria Visco, remembers those early days: "In September 1947 the Prima Maestra called me and gave me the job of starting up the apostolate of the cinema in collaboration with the Society of St Paul. Our first job was the selection of already existing films for reduction to 16mm for use in parish halls…

We also had to arrange for the distribution of these through agents; and then, still working with the Society of St Paul, we tried to produce original films covering religious education, catechetics and spiritual formation. I can say that I always found the Prima Maestra to be the true motivator of this apostolate… She encouraged us and offered us advice on the choice of films, and she was always telling us to chose only those films which were of real apostolic worth and which were concerned with true good of humanity… She often used to say: 'We need to do everything possible to carry the message of Christ into the world using the most expeditious and fruitful means so that it reaches the greatest number of people.'"

The Daughters also became involved in production: in the organisation of shooting, in the film printing laboratories and in distribution, and Thecla herself actually took the part of the prophetess Anna in the film *Mater Dei*.

The moment had arrived for the great undertaking: it was decided to produce a series of 50 catechetical documentaries, a kind of cinematic encyclopedia of Christianity characterised by a lively style of presentation, and designed to be shown all over the world. The cost would be enormous, and here the project ran into the usual difficulty: Fr Alberione did not have the money.

The whole thing had been the idea of the production company of the Society of St Paul, who accordingly ought to have paid for it themselves. But Thecla was not impressed by such distinctions: she was impatient of demarcations, of the bad feeling generated by the wish to possess, to exclude, to quarrel about trifles, which are the scourge of so many communities. For her, any Pauline project – whichever family might be managing it – was the concern of them all. This was 1951, and many people, as they had done 40 years before, thought Alberione was quite mad to be thinking about a programme for 50 documentaries; in spite of which, Thecla came forward with two-thirds of the sum needed for this Pauline, indeed this Catholic, enterprise.

Work was thus able to begin and the project was brought to a successful conclusion. For this timely intervention Maestra Thecla may rightly be regarded as a provident mother to the apostolate of the cinema.

But it was not only a great financial risk that Fr Alberione and Maestra Thecla had accepted when they embarked on this enterprise. To appreciate their courage from another point of view, it is well to recall that the project was blessed at its outset by Mgr Giovanni Battista Montini, Pope Pius XII's Pro-Secretary of State. Alberione had sent him the scripts of the 50 subjects to show to the Pontiff. Having done this, Mgr Montini wrote a letter on 19 January 1953 to Fr Alberione on behalf of Pius XII in which warm encouragement was tempered with ill-concealed anxiety. It is worth looking at this document again:

"This initiative could not fail to meet with a lively and paternal interest from the Holy Father, who always watches with confident attention over every experiment aimed at helping the great and important cause of the religious instruction of the young. If indeed the application of the techniques of the cinema to catechetical teaching were able to make it so lively, interesting and convincing as to form a benevolent link between the eternal truths and the learning capacity of children and of people at large, religious instruction would derive undoubted advantages from it... The Holy Father accordingly extends his good wishes to this delicate project, confident that every effort will be made to ensure that, from the doctrinal, artistic and administrative points of view it corresponds in practice with the good intentions which inspired it; and, in expressing his gratitude for this filial offering, he confers his blessing upon you, on all the members of the Pious Society and on the good and generous apostolic labours to which it is so wisely dedicated."

Apart from the encouragement and the blessing, this letter may be summed up very briefly: "Let's hope for the best!" For the moment this was the only reaction from the

Holy See to Fr Alberione, who had first had the idea, and to Maestra Thecla, the chief financial supporter of the enterprise.

Having completed and distributed the entire series of these documentaries, and seeing that they were so well received on all sides, Fr Alberione lost no time in making it known "in high places" that there was no longer any need to worry, even from an administrative point of view; and on the 28 May 1954, Giovanni Battista Montini conceded defeat with typically elegant wit: "The Supreme Pontiff was particularly pleased to hear your report about the progress achieved by the catechetical films, which have already enjoyed such widespread success in Italy and abroad. This enterprise cannot fail to make a truly important contribution to the cause of religious instruction." Not a word in the conditional now; everything in the indicative! The Founder and the Prima Maestra could summarise this letter too in very few words: "You were right!"

Help constantly available to everyone

To be ready to help everyone at any time: this was Thecla's guiding thought, and Fr Alberione testified to it after her death: "The Prima Maestra, directly and indirectly, not only with many prayers but in various forms and ways, contributed to the other institutions of the Pauline family... She had a great heart, modelled on the loving Heart of Jesus. She suffered the family's difficulties; she was gladdened by its growth; she kept herself well informed. In her last illness she remembered and prayed."

Fr Renato Perino added this note about the Founder's words: "These cursory remarks of Fr Alberione contain rather more than at first meets the eye. In that 'various forms and ways', in that 'great heart', in that 'suffered', 'gladdened' and so on we have only the outlines of his meaning, like rough sketches made by an old master for a portrait to be fleshed out by the hands of his pupils."

Work had already begun in 1945 on the great church to be dedicated to Mary Queen of Apostles in fulfilment of Fr Alberione's undertaking. The foundation stone was blessed in August 1947, and after three years the cross was placed on top of the cupola of this most impressive construction. The consecration and dedication took place in 1954 at the end of the Marian Year proclaimed by Pius XII, and the work was concluded in 1961.

Thecla had written to the Daughters in 1945 to ask them to assist with contributions towards the heavy expense; and she continued to remind them about this until it was finished and to suggest different ways in which they might help. She even asked the sick sisters to pray: "This church must be a monument to the activity and industry of us all."

The year 1953 was one of continuous journeys; there were three, running from spring through to autumn. The first, from 13 April to 22 May, was a return to the East, touching Japan, the Philippines and India. By now these visits were becoming part of the normal activity of management and were losing the exceptional character of the early days. They were also important for the members of both men's and women's Congregations: these more frequent personal contacts with the heads of their organisations ensured that they and their problems were better understood. It was one thing for them to write to Rome; it was quite another to speak directly to someone who had come specially from Rome to see them.

During this first journey, during a re-fuelling stop at Beirut, Maestra Thecla wrote home to the Daughters in Rome: "Here we are on the borders of Palestine, and the women dress just like Our Lady."

She also broke her journey to the East at Saigon in Vietnam, where she noted: "A group of soldiers boarded our plane at Saigon. I was very sorry for them; perhaps they were going to the war." The country had been occupied by the French during the nineteenth century and at that time was still known as Indochina. French troops under General

Salan were engaged in bitter fighting against the Vietminh guerrillas, the army of the independence movement.

How beautifully the young Japanese girls sang in the Daughters' chapel at Tokyo! As always, Thecla was enchanted by the Orient, or more precisely, by the people she met there. She noted with approval the excellent behaviour of the young people of Japan. The Daughters had their financial problems "just like in Rome", but she felt proud of this young community and of the Christian joy that suited those faces so well. (At this point the Prima Maestra's expressions of satisfaction must have caused her a slight interior tremor for she corrected herself immediately: "I'm sure that you pray for me, so that I shan't be an obstacle to grace for these Daughters.") And here she echoes a theme of Fr Alberione's: "We only know how to spoil things."

The cultural radio station was by now in full operation, and several of the Daughters were working there. Book centres had been opened at Osaka and Fukuoka and everything was proceeding in accord with the amiable disposition of these people: "The Daughters and the postulants are popular with everyone."

In the Philippines there was a most encouraging increase in vocations, and more demanding projects were being tackled; for example, the Days of the Divine Master and Gospel Days were attracting considerable attention.

Fr Alberione was taken ill during the visit to India. He suffered an eruption of the skin whilst he was at Allahabad and returned by train to Bombay, where Thecla arranged for him to be looked after in the house of the Daughters of St Paul. He remained there until he was ready to leave for Italy, on 25 May 1953.

On 13 July, less than two months later, the two superiors once again left together on another long journey, which took them to Canada, the United States, Colombia, Chile, Argentina and Brazil. They returned on 3 September.

They were received with the usual warmth by the priests and brothers of the Society, the Daughters and the Pious

Disciples, and there was the usual range of problems awaiting the Primo Maestro's decision. Maestra Thecla too had her quota of problems. She followed a somewhat different itinerary and was able to visit every one of the Daughters' houses and book centres.

Twenty one years had passed since the first two nuns arrived with 90 Lire in their pockets. The era of President Roosevelt had given way to the Presidency of Dwight D Eisenhower, and a World War had come and gone. Those pioneers had received reinforcement, and from modest beginnings they had developed their editorial, formative and apostolic work in new centres across the country. The Daughters had established themselves at Boston Massachusetts, Derby New York, Buffalo New York and Alexandria Louisiana.

Meanwhile in New York it became necessary to find a bigger house to accommodate the activities that the Daughters had started so long ago on Staten Island. Twenty years earlier they had had to make themselves appear small, harmless and almost invisible in order to be tolerated in certain dioceses. Now it was very different: the bishops begged them to come; they could never have enough Daughters of St Paul.

No complete account of this journey survives; however one feature emerges from diaries and other notes. James Alberione evidently endured considerable physical suffering: to the skin complaint first encountered in India was added the pain of rheumatism. He was unable to remain seated for long during the flights and he had to get up regularly to walk up and down the gangway, praying and reading his breviary. During the periods when he managed to stay in his seat he forced himself to write, in spite of the jolting of the aircraft.

Back on the ground, he immediately became immersed in his duties, saying Mass, preaching, visiting the existing houses, inspecting the sites for new ones. He paid particular attention on this journey to correcting the physical layout of some of these houses (of the Society, the Daughters and the Pious Disciples), laying down the arrangements to be followed in future. Every Pauline community had to have a residence of its own, separate from the others. However, they were not to be too widely scattered or to pursue their activities independently. They were to be close enough to operate as parts of a joint apostolate, open to all possible and acceptable forms of collaboration. It was also his hope that for every such group there should be a central church for the necessary occasions of common prayer.

"Our houses must be production lines of holy women"

Let us follow Maestra Thecla on her visits to the Daughters. She looks closely at everything, makes notes, points things out, corrects; and at the same time she is ready to help in the kitchen, to take the place of one of the Daughters in the book centre.

"We aren't all saints," she would say. But with her this is not a rebuke; it merely underlines a limitation shared by all; at the same time it is a reminder with an exceptional power to persuade and reassure. She used to tell the Daughters wherever she went that they were there to become holy. They could do that whether they succeeded or failed in the number of books they sold, whether or not they founded houses or started up new printing operations.

She insisted that the growth of the Pauline mission proceeded at God's chosen speed: his hand could not be forced. Personal holiness, on the other hand, was within the reach of them all. This thought lit up the path and strengthened the determination of all those Daughters of St Paul who walked miles every day and did other ordinary jobs for years on end without seeing any result. Thecla understood this perfectly: "We feel quite unequal to the task when we see the enormous amount of good there is to be done. But the Lord is with us: 'Do not fear; I am with you' is written in all our chapels. So let's have courage and trust in God! Our houses must be production lines of holy women."

They travelled on into Mexico, where the clothing took place of the first Mexican clerics to complete their formation in a Pauline house. On 6 August Fr Alberione made a short visit to Cuba. All that is known about this side-trip is that the Founder was received by the Archbishop of Havana and that he left for Colombia after a few hours. At Bogotà the Daughters were in the middle of their spiritual exercises and he was called on to give them a meditation. He later made it his business to speak to each of them alone, sisters, priests and brothers. The high altitude had increased his sufferings – he mentioned the fact to Thecla – and the celebration of Mass proved difficult and painful. However he was able to fulfil all his engagements and the visit proceeded according to plan until his return to Rome in early September.

This year of great journeys ended with a brief trip in November, when they visited France, Spain and Portugal.

Even defeat has its importance

In 1955, after sending so many sisters to open missions in faraway places, Thecla finally cast herself in the role of foundress. In the course of a journey with the Primo Maestro to the East (Philippines, Japan and India) she established the first presence of the Daughters of St Paul in Australia when she arrived there on 13 May. The two Superiors were accompanied on this extraordinary occasion by Maestra Redenta Commentucci and Sister Laurentia Casamassima to the Australian headquarters of the Paulines at Sydney. It was all a far cry from the furtive arrivals of former times. They were received in style by Cardinal Gilroy, with speeches of welcome in Italian. Religious communities offered them hospitality, and the sisters eventually established a house close to those of the Pauline priests and the Pious Disciples, who arrived later. Meanwhile the *Pastorelle*, the Sisters of Jesus the Good Shepherd, started a house at Melbourne.

This was a most gratifying journey. In Tokyo Thecla

found 105 Japanese Daughters of St Paul as well as dozens of novices and postulants. In the Philippines there were also over 100 Daughters; and in India there were three, with seven postulants. It was all very beautiful, but at the same time tragic. Young women were answering the call in every language and from all corners of the earth, and it was a cause for rejoicing when any girl agreed to follow Paul. But she could not lose sight of the millions of men and women who were far from Christ: "It breaks my heart!" she said. Yet progress was necessarily slow: Our Lord had to be presented to one person at a time. Their humble models must be the grain of mustard seed and the crib at Bethlehem.

And so she urged the Daughters – the two pioneers in Australia, the women of the Philippines, of Japan and that splendid little band in India – to take courage. True holiness took no account of material achievements; there were also prizes for failure. "So many times", she said, "a failure is a gift of God. We must find a place in our life for human failure and learn to be patient, however firm our intention of making ourselves holy. We must never lose heart; we must believe that everything is ordered for our good." 1955 was the Year of the Divine Master, dedicated to knowing, loving, imitating and praying to him. It was also the Year of the Holy Will of God, when – her notes tell us – she tried to imitate "Jesus the Master in his total acceptance of the will of his Father. Jesus is the Way. Imitate his examples, especially those of humility and mortification. Follow Jesus generously along the way of the Cross." These maxims, which we find as jottings in her spiritual notebooks, were the antidote to spiritual weariness for both herself and her Daughters.

The Philippine sisters had imported a brand new guillotine from Italy, and in the port of Manila the crate fell into the sea because of the clumsiness of the stevedores. Maestra Redenta wrote to Thecla expressing her "disgust" at the episode, and received this reply: "Why get so upset? It is less of a misfortune than a venial sin."

Whilst they were all together in Australia for the foundation of the house at Sydney, the Dominican sisters, whose guests they were, gathered round the Superior General to hear about the young Congregation. One sister exclaimed, full of admiration: "But you must be in charge of more than a thousand nuns and have more than a hundred houses to visit! You poor woman! What problems you must have!" The Prima Maestra let her finish; then with a broad smile and with great simplicity she replied: "Really, I don't do a thing. It's all the work of the good Lord; I just put my trust in him. But please pray for me, all of you!"

This was no ritual self-deprecation, a handy way of avoiding pointless discussion; it was the authentic Thecla. Her letters and notebooks of spiritual reflections are full of references to humility. It was the master-theme which ran through the symphony of her life, and fundamental to her self-analysis. By listening and reading, prayer and reflection she arrived at a proper understanding of humility: it was a struggle, not a refusal to fight; not a surrender, but a victory.

To become humble one needs strength, even assertive strength, as long as it remains under control. "Passion", she wrote, "is a strength: well-directed it can lead us to holiness. I am a very proud person, full of all manner of envy, jealousy and other faults. I want to make myself a saint, a great saint. I must never lose sight of my wretchedness; the more I am humiliated, the more must I humiliate myself."

Several Daughters of St Paul remember how they felt ill at ease on first meeting the Prima Maestra on account of her austere appearance, her calm and very controlled manner. But sooner or later there would be a flash of joy in those eyes and the Thecla of serene humility would take over from the woman of strength. She was a living example of "well-directed passion", making it flow in the direction of holiness.

In September 1953 there was a meeting in Rome of the National Council of Superiors General, an organisation created to promote understanding and co-operation among orders and congregations, and Maestra Thecla – in her absence – was elected president of the newly-constituted FIRAS, the Italian federation of women religious working in the field of community care. She could scarcely believe the news and her first reaction was to check it: "Perhaps there has been a mistake." To be asked to hold any office outside the Pauline world was the last thing she ever expected. However, she performed her new duties with the same efficiency as all her others.

One of the problems she had to resolve concerned nuns who taught in infant schools. The FIRAS council had to decide about starting a specialised course for them, finding the right people to run it, the right place to hold it and finding money to pay for it. An expert in this field stated bluntly that the idea was impracticable, and everyone looked to Thecla for guidance. She asked only one question: Did the Congregation of Religious consider this an important course? On receiving an affirmative reply she made an immediate decision in the style of Fr Alberione: "Then the course simply must be organised. Let us do everything we can and the Lord will help us." Maestra Ignazia Balla, her successor as Superior General, remembered: "The course was held; many students took part, and it was an unexpected success. Others like it were organised in successive years, and the sisters who attended derived great benefit from it."

In the turmoil of the coup d'état

"I still carry in my mind and heart the memory of the progress I observed in vocations, in the apostolate and in the great religious spirit which animates our South American sisters."

These words of encouragement are a typical extract from one of the "bulletins" that she used to write following her overseas visits. This one commented on the second of her 1955 journeys, when she and Fr Alberione were accompanied by Mother Lucia Ricci, the Superior General of the

Pious Disciples. It was the customary tour of the American houses: the United States, Canada, Mexico, Colombia, Chile, Argentina and Brazil, and included some unscheduled changes to the itinerary. On the way out they stopped over in London to look at the newly-opened house of the Daughters under Maestra Rosaria Visco. This apostolate had made rapid progress because books in English already existed, printed by the Pauline priests and brothers in London and the United States. Fr Alberione gave the instructions already referred to for the disposition of the houses of the Pauline foundation to be built at Langley, not far out of London.

In New York the Prima Maestra found that 18 postulants had joined the Daughters – "something never seen in America!". Moreover, the noviciate at Boston was almost completed, and they were preparing to open up on the Pacific coast with a house at San Diego in California.

Both in Canada and Colombia the houses were proving too small and extensions were approved. In Colombia it was proving difficult to attract vocations. "In Argentina the Daughters passed a few rather frightening days, but they were not greatly inconvenienced." Thecla was referring here to the military coup d'état by members of the naval high command, who in September 1955 succeeded in toppling the dictator Juan Peròn. She continues: "*Familia Cristiana* has reached 112,000 copies, and it is the only Catholic periodical that wasn't suppressed during the Peròn persecution. The experience has made those dear sisters even more zealous and more deeply committed to their vocation."

Once again on this journey Fr Alberione made a brief visit to Cuba. This was a more public occasion, with journalists, photographers and television in attendance at Havana airport. There was a meeting with Cardinal Arteaga y Betancourt, an official reception and speeches of thanks. There was a request for reinforcements for the Pauline priests and brothers, who are already installed on the island.

The Primo Maestro accepted gladly all suggestions for concrete action, and where none were forthcoming he took action himself; or so we are led to suppose from a note by Mother Lucia Ricci of the Pious Disciples: "The Primo Maestro, as usual, prays a great deal, works very hard, rests far too little and is not in the best of health. But wherever he goes he awakens fresh energies, prompts new initiatives and gives new life to projects already under-way."

In Cuba and Venezuela there were requests for "the sisters with the books", but Thecla could not respond to the need immediately: "Where on earth can I find them?"

So at last her Daughters were in demand, and people were even crying out for them; the revolution begun by Thecla Merlo of Castagnito, with her girls and Fr Alberione had finally triumphed. They had come a long way since the suspicions and subterfuges of Alba, the camouflaged activities in the women's workshop, the semi-clandestine operation at Susa, fearing the disapproval even of sacristans. Now they had finally come into their own, fêted by bishops and cardinals at almost every landfall.

It would have been natural and entirely justified if, forty years after making her first commitment in Canon Chiesa's sacristy, the unschooled seamstress who was considered too sickly for the Cottolengo sisters, had shown some signs of satisfaction. But to indulge in such thoughts would have been a waste of time and, as the Primo Maestro used to point out, a sin against poverty. In any case, there was a proper time for satisfaction; this began at the instant of death and not an instant before. Until then the chief benefit to be derived from life's experiences was to learn from them.

The lesson that Thecla learned from her American journey of 1955 was this: "In all the houses and in every country, I have found so much fervour, such zeal for the many plans for the apostolate and a great affection for the Superiors of the Congregation. For these Daughters, every instruction that comes from Rome is the word of the Gospel; and everyone sincerely wants to make progress, convinced that affection for Rome brings unity and peace in the Congregation and promotes the growth of its works. I thank the Divine Master, the Queen of the Apostles and our Father St Paul for the many beautiful things I have seen."

"Let no one draw back from the challenge!"

During this journey she was thinking about two editorial projects which were typical of the Daughters' output. One was a catechetical magazine: *Via, Verità e Vita* (The way, the truth and the life), which had first been launched in 1952 – about the same time as *La vita in Cristo e nella Chiesa* (Life in Christ and in the Church) was started by the Pious Disciples. The other was a brave attempt to produce a modern women's magazine based on Christian principles and directed to the younger generation. When she left for the Americas the name had not yet been chosen. It eventually came out on 25 December 1955 under the title *Così* (Like this!). For eleven years it occupied a worthy, indeed a unique, position in the international Catholic press.

Maestra Thecla threw herself heart and soul into this enterprise, even whilst she was on her travels. On 12 September she wrote in haste during the flight to Paris: "About the magazine which is about to come out, it would be a good idea to make a novena to the Most Blessed Virgin for its success, to pray that it grows rapidly to become an influence for good; in these modern times we need to be quick off the mark."

And the next day: "I recommend the new magazine to all of you. It is very close to my heart for there is so much good to be done among young women. You must all be involved; this new title is everyone's business."

She returns to the subject again in October. The new magazine, she says, "must be prepared in prayer", like every project of the Pauline family. She then reminds them: "The launch of the new title ought not to be simply accepted as another job, but welcomed with enthusiasm. The Primo

Maestro has said that a magazine of this type will be good for the Congregation; it will be a means of attracting vocations and will help to guide the studies of its readers." But how was a new publication to be launched without an advertising budget? "Let's begin by talking about it among ourselves; speak of it in the book centres; think of all the possible methods of getting it into colleges, institutes and parishes." But above all, "let no one draw back from the challenge, saying, 'It isn't my business; I work in the cinema,' or 'I work in the house.' We must all of us be involved. I want to do my part with you. Wherever I go I talk about it and ask for prayers for its success. Have no fear!"

As regards *Via, Verità e Vita*, she was glad to note that the title was doing so well in Italy, that a French version was to be launched in Paris and Canada, and that Spanish and Portuguese editions would shortly be circulating in Latin America.

In the last days of July 1956 she made the only journey of the year: to the United Kingdom and to Spain, where a new house had recently been founded in Madrid. Here the Primo Maestro considered the merits of various sites for a permanent establishment in view of the prospect of future developments.

Towards the end of the year the Prima Maestra and her Councillors began preparations for an event of great importance in the life of the Congregation, the first General Chapter in the history of the Daughters of St Paul.

Chapter Seven

HARVEST TIME

The General Chapter is the supreme legislative body of every religious institute. The first one is normally summoned when a congregation has reached a significant size and achieved a certain stability, and it usually consists of the major superiors currently in office together with elected delegates. Such were the arrangements for the Society of the Daughters of St Paul when their first General Chapter was held in 1957.

Maestra Thecla issued the notice of convocation in January, naming the superiors who would participate as of right, and the method of electing delegates. The venue was to be the Generalate in Rome and the Chapter would run from 4 to 7 May, following a week's retreat.

However, on 20 February she had very different news to announce: "A greeting to you all to say that I know you will be praying for me. On Saturday 23, I am to have a small operation. This is just to let you know why I won't be able to write to you for a little while." But this was not to be a small operation. Her health had always been delicate, but on top of her usual troubles she had been feeling pain in one breast and the outcome of the examination was the one everyone most feared: she needed an immediate radical mastectomy. Everything was done "at home", at the *Regina Apostolorum* clinic for religious at Albano Laziale in the hills south of Rome. This was another of Fr Alberione's ideas which Thecla had brought to fruition a few years after the war. She had always been a member of the family here, making frequent visits to the sick of both her own and other congregations, and she made sure that there was a special place reserved for the Benedictines of Montecassino and for the nuns of other enclosed orders.

The surgery carried out by Professor Ojetti was both timely and effective; he later recalled: "When we performed the operation for cancer of the breast all my colleagues remarked how cruel it was that she of all people should have been singled out for such a fate. But she remained her usual matter-of-fact self, and was impatient of all sympathy, 'You will do what you must.'"

Short bulletins to the Daughters announced the successful outcome and the progress of her convalescence. Meanwhile, the General Chapter took place at the appointed time, and on 4 May she was unanimously reconfirmed in the office of Superior General.

One of her circulars in the early summer shows that she was still actively concerned with the business of her religious family and ready to step in when any lack of dedication was brought to her notice. Her method is characteristically indirect: she refers to a variety of shortcomings, leaving it to the reader's intuition to decide precisely what and who are being referred to. She recalls that "we ought not to judge, but to love; not to resist, but to become ever more meek and compliant in accepting the duties of office and the instructions of others." She also notes that obedience brings its own rewards: "The most obedient among the Daughters of St Paul are also the most content, whilst those who do not obey willingly – who do not submit generously to orders – live troubled lives, become irritable, and eventually infect others with their own discontent." It is as though she is looking at them one by one, these Daughters that she so much wants to become holy. That is why she cannot allow certain shortcomings to pass unnoticed: there is always time to change course; improvement is within the reach of everyone. And of course she accuses herself of much worse when she examines her own conscience.

There were no foreign journeys in 1957 and 1958. She was still very weak, though she began gradually to resume her duties, including the presidency of FIRAS. She had intended to go to the Philippines in 1958, but in the end her

Vicar General, Maestra Ignazia Balla, took her place.

On 9 October 1958, Pope Pius XII died at Castelgandolfo at the age of 82. Less than three weeks later, the 76-year-old Angelo Giuseppe Roncalli was presented to a slightly surprised world as John XXIII, inaugurating a pontificate which would bring about important changes. He had not been long on the throne when, one cold winter morning in the Roman basilica of St Paul, he announced the greatest initiative of the century in the Catholic Church: the second Ecumenical Council of the Vatican. Fr Alberione was quick to comment: "He is the Pope for these times."

Thecla resumes her travels

In September 1959 Thecla left for a five-month tour of the Americas. Her health was still uncertain and she had to take long rests after each flight. This time Fr Alberione was not with her: she was accompanied by Mother Lucia Ricci, the Superior of the Pious Disciples. Over the United States their flight path crossed that of the Soviet leader Nikita Khruschev, who was visiting President Eisenhower. During these flights she was unable to write as she was accustomed to do, but she assured the Daughters – or at least that was her intention – when she wrote from Boston: "I am fairly well; you mustn't worry about me; I am very well looked after and I have all the help I need."

The longer stopovers of this journey allowed her to look more closely than usual at the work being done and above all to spend more time with each of the Daughters. She greatly valued these opportunities of speaking to them face to face and of listening to what they had to say. It was some time since she had been able to fulfil a duty she had long regarded as fundamental – replying in person to the letters she regularly received from her sisters. Now she was able to speak to each in turn as she moved through the United States, Canada, Mexico, Venezuela, Colombia, Chile, Argentina and Brazil.

In all the houses the problem was the same as ever, the shortage of Daughters in comparison with the work to be done. But this had not prevented the grain of mustard seed from growing. Despite their insufficient numbers the Daughters were giving a good account of themselves. The prospects in Venezuela were particularly good, whilst the premises occupied in various centres, including Caracas and Bogota, were already proving too small. She was amazed at the vastness of the Argentinean pampas, where the Daughters were also making progress, evidenced by the newest house of the Congregation at Mendoza.

In many places she saw a great catechetical movement developing, which needed active support from the centre. She was quick to point this out to the Daughters on her return to Rome: "The Daughters [on the overseas missions] copy much of what we do here and they depend on us; it's up to us to think of new ideas and methods to help our sisters abroad."

She met many bishops and parish priests who asked her to send more Daughters, which made her think back to the hostile reception reserved for them in former times. But she also remembered what Fr Alberione said about these rejections: "It doesn't matter: the day will arrive when they will implore you to come and you will no longer be able to go everywhere they want you." This was just what was happening now, and Thecla pointed it out to the sisters in Rome to underline both the necessity and the wisdom of obedience. "This shows that what the Primo Maestro says will be fulfilled to the letter, provided we follow his instructions."

In Colombia *Sampaolo Film* had made a promising start. At Curitiba in Brazil the Daughters were recording their catechism lessons on tape for transmission by the small radio transmitter of the diocese. "They would like more radio stations there, but that's impossible for technical reasons." Thecla's reply, and her subsequent persistence, was in the Alberionian manner: "Make gramophone records of those lessons, and then you will be able to broadcast them everywhere!" Which was all very well, but how were they to make records at a place like Curitiba? "But why not at Curitiba?" was her reply. They had a small amount of equipment. They would probably make mistakes at the beginning, but then everyone did. Good ideas did not have to come from Rome, but could be dreamed up and be put into practice anywhere. As she was leaving the next day she again insisted that they should try to make their own recordings, and indeed discs were eventually produced at Curibita. Their success led in due course to the establishment of a production centre at São Paulo.

Things like this were happening in every community, often without becoming known to others and with the risk that they would eventually be forgotten with the death or transfer of those involved. So Thecla, before returning to Italy, sent out one of her circulars suggesting that all the overseas houses should write their histories, describing their beginnings and how they overcame their various problems. "I think this is a useful exercise; and if it isn't done now I'm sure we shall regret it later. Who knows what ideas will come to light."

For all vocations

"You ought to stock the new magazine *Se vuoi...* (If you want...) in all the book centres and do your best to promote it. It is published by the Queen of Apostles Sisters, the *Apostoline*, which as you know is one of the congregations of the Pauline family." This quotation comes from a circular dated 12 March 1960.

This new community had been founded in 1957 to encourage and support vocations of any and every kind, for whatever order, congregation or institute. Fr Alberione described its scope with words of typical broad sweep and vigour: "All Catholics, with all their forces, by every means, for all vocations, for every apostolate." It was something he had long had in mind, even in the days of pious self-interest when a priest sent to the missions was sometimes seen as a pastor stolen from the diocese. The original intention was that the *Apostoline* should be an informal community. Later it seemed better for the group to be modelled along the lines of a religious institute. The first step was taken when, in September 1959, the first seven members made their profession of vows.

Maestra Thecla was quick to appreciate the value of this initiative even though it deprived her of several future Daughters of St Paul. This was not simply a matter of obedience to the Primo Maestro but a case of complete harmony of vision, based on her personal experience of many years.

One of the first members of the new Congregation was Maddalena Verani, a young woman whose home was not far from the General house. She was well known to the Prima Maestra, who in the past had given help to her family, and Thecla was overjoyed to learn that she had decided to join the Daughters of St Paul. However, one day the girl spoke to Fr Alberione: "He told me quite plainly that he thought I was better suited to the new group which was to form the new Institute of the Queen of Apostles, the mission for vocations, rather than to the Daughters of St Paul. And when I asked, fearing her disappointment, that the Prima Maestra should be told of this she let me know immediately that she was more than happy with the Primo Maestro's advice to me. On the eve of my admission to the new Congregation she gave me a beautiful parcel of linen for my trousseau."

Soon afterwards Thecla visited the sisters in their small house at Castelgandolfo, bringing them the present of a tape recorder so that they could play back the conferences of Fr Alberione.

It never occurred to her that Fr Alberione was taking too much on, starting too many organisations. On the contrary she was fascinated by his integrated vision, the way in which his many charisms worked together. She was not one to concern herself too much about material means or the human instruments of whom only so much could be asked. Her sole worry was that the faith of her Daughters might be lukewarm, their prayer not confident enough. One day she received a letter from the superior of the Japanese house who was worried by serious financial problems. She replied by pointing out the heavy indebtedness of the Generalate and concluded with these words: "We really don't know which way to turn; so we'll turn to the tabernacle and somehow help will arrive. You should try to have the same trust."

"Come away to a lonely place"

In the summer of 1960 she took the cure at the spa town of Chianciano in central Italy, making the most of the opportunity to intensify her prayers for the Daughters: "I have time to pray here and I regularly manage three or four hours a day. We have so much need of prayer and I remember the whole Congregation."

In 1960 she began to reduce her schedule of visits to the establishments of the Congregation outside Italy. She went to the United Kingdom in August to see the new house at Langley, and in September she visited the Daughters in Madrid.

The Founder was also thinking about the prayer life of the Society – and with his usual breadth of vision. He felt that a new and fertile period was beginning: for the Church as a whole in the Ecumenical Council, and for the Pauline family with its growing presence on every continent. It seemed an appropriate moment for them to pause, to pray for new energy and to reflect on their personal and collective sense of direction. He accordingly decided that all Pauline priests and brothers should perform a month of spiritual exercises every few years. They would be following Jesus' recommendation to his Apostles when they returned from their preaching missions: "Come away to a lonely place, and rest a while" (Mk 6:31).

These exercises first took place in April 1960 in the Pauline house of the Divine Master at Ariccia, just south of Rome in the Alban Hills, and they ended with a papal audience. This was the first time that the Society of St Paul was received as a body by the new Vicar of Christ. He asked them to pray for the objectives of the Council and of his pontificate, adding: "The works of the Society of St Paul… are destined to honour the Eighth Commandment which, of all the Lord's Commandments is the one which today stands in greatest danger. You see how untruth lies at the bottom of relations between man and man. All the world's troubles come down to a betrayal of truth."

The Daughters also had three weeks of special spiritual exercises. In May 1961, Fr Alberione gathered together everyone who had been in the Congregation from the beginning, along with all those currently in office or with responsibility for spiritual formation. And it was then that Thecla, during this period of total concentration "in a lonely place", made an act of complete dedication. On 15 May, the feast of the Most Holy Trinity, she offered her life for the sanctification of the Daughters of St Paul; in other words she signified her acceptance of death at any moment as long as it served that purpose. Clearly, she also wanted her sisters to be effective apostles, publishers, writers, up-to-date experts in all forms of social communications, but always – as the Constitutions themselves lay down – as a secondary objective. Their first and most important objective remained personal sanctification, and Thecla's chief task was to school them for greatness in the spiritual life. Deeply though she loved her religious family, she never forgot that it was only a means, to be rigorously subordinated to this final end. In the notebook of her personal meditations she warns: "Don't put the Congregation before the Lord. Perfection consists of doing the will of God."

She had now made many journeys, but she had still to visit Africa, where the Daughters were also established. In June 1958 Maestra Basilia Bianco and Sister Giuseppa Panarello arrived in Zaire, which was then still known as the Belgian Congo. They established themselves in the capital city, Leopoldville, today's Kinshasa, and in the following year opened a branch house in Elizabethville, now Lubumbashi, the principal town of the province of Katanga. Shortly after independence in July 1960, Moise Tshombe assumed power in Katanga, the most prosperous area of Zaire, and declared its secession from the new state. Civil war immediately followed. In February 1961 the prime minister of Zaire, Patrice Lumumba, was assassinated, and in September Dag Hammarskjøld, Secretary-General of the United Nations, was killed in an air crash whilst on his way to meet Tshombe to negotiate a truce. It was against this blood-stained background that Maestra Thecla made her visit in early November 1961.

She had to content herself with a visit to the Daughters in the capital; those in Katanga could not be reached because the civil war was still raging. The small group of sisters, however, remained at their posts in accordance with Pauline tradition, and Thecla gave this account of them in a circular to the Congregation: "The sisters in Africa greet you all! They are happy and they are doing much good work there. It is quite true that Africa casts a particular spell, and it is touching to see so many people thirsty for God's word. Let us help them with prayer and small daily sacrifices. When I look at the poverty that afflicts so many of them I am almost ashamed to think that we religious, despite our own vow of poverty, live in the lap of luxury."

Despite her condition, she was determined to make one more visit to the East. She was sure she could manage as long as she took one of the Daughters with her as secretary to lighten the burden of correspondence. The itinerary was the now familiar one of India, the Philippines, Japan, and Australia, but with the addition of South Korea and Taiwan. She left on 24 January 1962 and she was back in Rome by 19 May. Once again she took care to pause between flights so as not to tire herself too much. "I am well; don't worry about me," she wrote from Bombay. And as always she observed and studied the people. The East was not just a landscape, but a panorama of faces, expressions, individual people: "In this great country of India one feels so very, very small – like a grain of dust."

During her stay in the Philippines she began to feel less well, and she was in tears as she read the letters sent by the Daughters. "I am feeling the effect of this climate; it drains my strength." Indeed she fell ill at Pasay City, and Maestra Costantina Bignante had to rush out from Italy to act as nurse and personal assistant. But Thecla did not abandon the journey. She probably realised that she was passing this way for the last time and that she would have to say to the sisters, like the Apostle, "you will see my face no more" (Acts 20:25). But she made little of her sufferings and treated them as unimportant.

It was the same when she visited her people at Castagnito d'Alba, where she was as reticent about her problems as she was about her achievements. Thecla, her brothers and their families all came from the same solid but undemonstrative tradition in which people may love each other very dearly all their lives without ever once saying so.

She usually managed to fit in a visit to the family whenever she went to the house at Alba, but it was never treated as anything exceptional. As Fr Costanzo Leone recalled: "For all of her brothers she was simply our sister Teresa; for her nephews and nieces she was 'great Teresa' – as aunts used to be called in the Piedmontese dialect – who wore no halo, and who sometimes brought them sweets and chocolates. We had a very general idea of her journeys and of her work in the various houses, but when she came to stay with the family for a short break it seemed as though she hadn't a worry in the world. She enjoyed the company of her young nephews and nieces, who told her all about their little problems as if she had nothing more important to think about." She would often appear without warning: "I was just passing by, so I thought I would call and say hello." They would ask her if she had been to any far-away places, and she might reply that she had just returned from Japan and had had a good journey. But conversation about the wider world was quickly exhausted, and she soon became 'great Teresa' again, anxious to hear the news of Castagnito and its people. "My brothers and I were chiefly struck by her utter simplicity and her total peace of mind. We never once saw her angry or even sad."

She was anything but sad on her return from the East in May, when she went to speak to the sisters who had gathered at Ariccia for their spiritual exercises. As usual, she spoke as though to an informal family gathering. She described how, when their plane developed a fault on the ground at Bombay and the air conditioning failed "it was as though we were in an oven", yet the Daughters of St Paul appeared not to feel any discomfort. "And I thought at the time: it must be because their hearts are full of the love of God. For when we have God's love within us, that warms us so much that we hardly notice the heat outside. I really believe that's how it was."

The Gospel Days in the Philippines were a great success, and even more gratifying was the number of vocations from among those remarkable people, the first to send missionaries to other countries. The situation in Japan was completely different; most of the people were not even Christians. "We might meet perhaps one or two Catholics in a day's work ... but how eagerly they bought the gospels and our other books!" It is wonderful to imagine these "far-away people" at the moment of their first contact with Jesus – for example when they opened the gospels and they heard for the first time the recital of the Beatitudes.

Maestra Thecla undoubtedly experienced the same

overwhelming joy as the disciples of St Paul when they saw the first signs of interest in the Good News about Jesus of Nazareth, crucified and risen. She was not the sort to regard "the deposit of faith" as something so precious that it had to be locked away for protection. For her, the best way of keeping the faith was to preach it to "the pagans", as she called non-Christians; otherwise God's Word was reduced to so many buried talents. The seamstress from Castagnito, standing amid the mass of Eastern humanity, was profoundly aware of the problem of the Church's apostolic mission as it was to be formulated many years later by an eminent theologian:

"It is not just a matter of our being able to guarantee the truthfulness of evidence about Christ by referring to a written document that tells us what the Apostles saw and said. The Church has a continuing relationship with the Apostles through all time... And so the Church is most truly apostolic when it is looking towards the future, for the message entrusted to us is not only about things that have already happened but also about events that are yet to come. Within the apostolic framework the Church feels a characteristic tension as it tries to re-live the old truths in the context of an evolving present. No church could be considered apostolic which was concerned essentially with its future and forgot its points of reference in the past. And the same would be true of a church so preoccupied with its origins as to be incapable of making its message relevant to successive ages." (S Dianich, *La Chiesa mistero di comunione* [The Church, a mystery of communion] Ed Paoline)

Maestra Thecla described her visit to Taiwan, where the Congregation had started work in 1959 at the request of the local Church authorities. The house had been opened by Sister Donata Bugnola, and she had been reinforced from the Philippines by Sister Costanza Justo, Sister Giovanna Abuda and Sister Timotea Villaram. The Daughters arrived in South Korea in 1960 with Maestra Eulalia d'Ettorre and Sister Lidia Meggiolaro along with two Japanese Daughters of St Paul. "We are all one great family," exclaimed Maestra Thecla. "We are sisters all Daughters of St Paul and we come from all over the world."

Only small progress had been possible in Taiwan; the sisters were still struggling with the Chinese language. As for Korea, "O poor Korea! They have little of this world's goods, but they are rich in spirit." The country had barely emerged from the horrors of a war that had killed a million non-combatants and left a similar number of homeless refugees. Yet they seemed not to complain. They were already working with great efficiency, though their true industrial revolution was still some years away.

The Christians were a small minority, but they had a history of unique persistence and courage. Christianity had been brought to Korea by a layman in the eighteenth century, and from this beginning a more or less clandestine community of a few thousand souls had flourished without benefit of ordained ministers. A Chinese priest visited them in 1794, but he was killed almost immediately. At that time the country was a vassal province of the Chinese Empire and as such it was closed to all foreign influence. Thirty years later a French missionary died of exhaustion in Mongolia whilst on a secret journey to visit the isolated flock. At last another Frenchman succeeded in getting through, but he in turn was killed three years later, along with several of the faithful. Despite these extraordinary privations the Church somehow managed to survive in Korea.

The people Thecla met were the descendants of these extraordinary Christians. "We were in a church in Seoul. The parish priest had no curate. He celebrated three Masses; preached three sermons, and then he had all the various parish activities to manage. But you should have seen the spirit and fervour of the man! He seemed to combine the qualities of the early Christians with those of the Curé of Ars." With men like him to guide the faithful it was natural that vocations should follow.

The second Ecumenical Council of the Vatican opened in Rome in October 1962. St Peter's Square and the surrounding area was ablaze with the purple, red and gold ceremonial robes of the assembled dignitaries. Patriarchs of the Eastern Churches mingled in a colourful throng of bishops from every corner of the earth. These successors of the Apostles, summoned by Pope John to a truly universal assembly, represented widely different conditions of life. There was Enrique Play Deniel, the Cardinal Archbishop of Seville, a city where the beacon of Christianity had shone brightly for the last 1,300 years. But there was also the African bishop who habitually went barefoot about his enormous diocese. Cardinal Francis Spellman of New York governed a See of a million and a half Catholics with the help of nine auxiliary bishops, whilst Georges Xenopoulos, Bishop of Candia, could care for his 320 Catholics and his three priests without resort to pastoral letters – he could speak personally to them all. There was a bishop from the region of the Sahara, who lived as a beggar. There were poor bishops from every continent and among them Italian bishops from small dioceses.

Many of them knew of the Daughters of St Paul and called at the Generalate to greet Maestra Thecla. She received them graciously and, thanks to reports from her Daughters, she was already aware of their predicament. Some had only one pair of shoes; many were already suffering from the chill of Rome's October weather. They went through secret agonies to hide their difficulties, refusing invitations and wondering how they were going to manage if the Council went on for a long time.

The marvellous poverty of so many of the Fathers was one of the least noted features of the Ecumenical Council, but Thecla was as solicitous in arranging for the material welfare of these men as she had been in helping the priests and brothers of the Society in their hour of need.

Sister Nazarena Morando recalls those days: "When the bishops began to arrive, particularly those from the mission territories and the developing countries, the Prima Maestra's first thought was to ensure that they had enough warm clothes for the winter. Naturally enough, many who came from tropical countries had no woollen garments at all..."

Thecla organised help for them, beginning with the Daughters themselves, who offered their own new woollens, and she later approached families and clothing manufacturers for donations. With great discretion, she obtained information about the wardrobes of some of the visiting bishops – from their surplices to their socks – and discovered that many of them were driven to heroic improvisations to conceal the shame of their need. She was thus able to ensure that help was given where it was most needed, as she had done during the war. In some cases she gave them a small sum of money: "For a coffee... and the tram..."

Sister Nazarena recalls another detail: "She even arranged for two sisters to drive round each week to collect their personal linen from the hotels and boarding houses, so that even the poorest bishops had an efficient laundry service for the duration of the Council. Many superiors of the Daughters of St Paul in their far-flung missions heard of this kindness of their Mother General only when their bishop came to thank them on his return from Rome. I mention that this service continued until the end of the Council because after the Prima Maestra's death we carried on the work with the same dedication that she had taught us."

Christmas 1962, the first of the Council, was a period of easy-going euphoria. Pope John spoke of looking for ways of bringing about Christian unity, and for many people it seemed that unity was within easy reach and would be achieved at no great cost.

This was not Thecla's view; she was only too aware of the problems. Her Christmas circular was confident, but also realistic. She had some serious points to make which could not be glossed over.

She had noticed in various places a certain temptation to individualism, due in part to the nature of the Daughters' mission: a tendency to consider as personal achievements work that in reality stood to the credit of the whole Congregation. This all came back to a failure of sisterly love. It was all very well to talk about Christian unity, "but the first unity we must achieve is among ourselves – to love, to forgive and to share with one another... I'm afraid I see signs of a damaging tendency at work. There are those whose hearts are not as dedicated to the Congregation as they ought to be and who think of their own interests before those of the Institute... It makes me sad to hear talk of 'them' and 'us'. We are all 'us', with a single heart and soul!"

She ended by urging her sisters to accept all the Congregation's policies and directives "generously and in their entirety", and exhorted them to offer up their obedience for the intentions of the Council – in particular so that everyone would gladly accept its decisions.

Though she was deeply concerned about this threat to the Institute, she was also keenly aware of the extraordinary sacrifices accepted by Daughters throughout the world and she was anxious that they should not go unnoticed. Many of these were worth writing about and bringing to the attention of others. There were also many Daughters who completed 25 years in the religious life in 1963. She thanked them publicly in her circular of 10 January: "May the good Lord be praised for the graces he has given to each of you. The Congregation is also grateful to you for the fine work you have done and for the example of virtue and dedication during all these years."

Her thoughts went out to the Daughters of St Paul in Katanga and Lubumbashi, caught in the middle of a guerrilla war and cut off from their sisters in the capital, Kinshasa. They had been forced to suspend all apostolic work and were finally driven from their house to seek refuge as best they could. They found a temporary home with the

Sisters of Charity of Ghent before settling into premises placed at their disposal by a mining company. There they were visited by Maestra Ignazia Balla, Thecla's Vicar General, who managed to spend some time with them after an adventurous journey. There they remained until the situation returned to normal; whereupon they immediately opened a centre which soon became the most popular bookshop in the city.

Thecla was by now beginning to feel a little better, and on hearing the improved news from the Congo she decided that she would go there herself, overruling the objections of the many who advised her to be more prudent. She left on 8 May 1963 and returned after ten days. It was to be her last overseas journey.

She had witnessed the fire at the tiny printing shop at Susa and she remembered the bombs that landed by the General house during the war. She had comforted the sisters who were swept up in the war in China, in the invasion of the Philippines and in the Argentinean *coup d'état*. Now she felt she simply had to visit her Daughters in Africa and to embrace them in their own city, in their own book centre. But this final journey of the Prima Maestra had none of the melancholy flavour of a farewell; she was going to congratulate her valiant followers, and the "decorations" she would distribute were the stocks of books to replace those destroyed during the conflict.

Sister Elena Ramondetti recalled that "at the end she seemed especially maternal towards everyone else and yet she continued to be hard on herself. She had a great spirit of self-denial, and demonstrated this by insisting on obedience to the rule and carrying out all the observances of the community. Though she was often tired from her many engagements she liked to spend as much time as possible among her Daughters. At recreation times she enjoyed nothing better than simply being among them and talking to them; and this was her way whether she was in Rome at the Generalate or away on a visit."

When she finally ceased to travel, the Generalate became her whole world, and though she now wrote fewer letters she continued the brief daily entries in her spiritual notebook. She became gradually less concerned with the problems of a Superior General, and the notes eventually became the diary of the soul of Thecla Merlo of the Daughters of St Paul.

2 June 1963: "Live in the grace and under the guiding hand of the Holy Spirit. He is the one who works within my soul. The Father and the Son are with him. Never forget the Holy Spirit; he is the one who makes us holy."

3 June 1963: "Live in union with God like St Paul: 'For to me to live is Christ' (Phil 1:21). Do everything for him, in him, with him. Love souls and do good works. May all mankind be saved! Always humility, patience and faith. Mary help me!"

Pope John XXIII died on the evening of 3 June and she notes the event the following day: "Yesterday the Pope passed away at 7.49 pm. Always be ready for God's call. Do everything to please him and Mary most holy. Be kind to everyone. *Requiem…*"

5 June 1963: "Be constantly aware of eternity. Life is the preparation for heaven. Do everything for God alone. Mary, I trust in you."

6 June 1963: "Burial of our Holy Father Pope John XXIII. Love, practise humility, mortify the self. Observance of vows – poverty, obedience, delicacy. Everything with a view to eternity. Mary, I trust in you."

16 June 1963: "Full confidence in Jesus my saviour, who died for me, that he will open for me the way to paradise. He showed me his love by calling me to the religious life. My Jesus, I put all my trust in you!"

On the same day that she wrote this note she suffered a stroke. So began the period of sickness which ended with her death eight months later.

On the following day Thecla could only write, "Don't understand much – ill," and the next day "Ditto". The entry for 19 June was just one word: "ILL", but two days later she recorded feeling better, and on the 26th she wrote, "Do what is pleasing to God. Have great faith in him."

The diary entries continue until 22 November and close with these words: "Lord, I want to do your will always and in all things; to obey you always and in all things. My Guardian Angel, help me!"

Eight thousand letters

She had suffered her first stroke on a Sunday, a day when no *Angelus* bell rang in St Peter's Square because of the vacant papal throne. It was still five days from the election of Giovanni Battista Montini as Paul VI on Friday June 21. Thecla had two engagements that day. In the morning she was to meet a group of novices in the Divine Master house at Ariccia, and in the afternoon after vespers she had a meeting of her Council at nearby Albano Laziale at the *Regina Apostolorum* hospital, where she was then staying.

She managed to complete the day's programme, though with increasingly evident difficulty. During the morning she complained of stomach pains and exhaustion; in the afternoon and evening she had difficulty in speaking, concentration was evidently a problem. She went to bed immediately after supper. She tried to speak but could only repeat, "Yes... yes... poor thing!... if I can't manage it doesn't matter..."

She began to retch. The doctor was sent for and he diagnosed a stroke with possible thrombosis. By 11 o'clock she had lost consciousness and Fr Dragone, the clinic chaplain, was called to give her the Sacrament of the Sick. He remembers the occasion well: "I anointed her in the presence of all the Superiors of the General Council and of her Vicar General, Maestra Ignazia Balla, and I also gave her the apostolic blessing with plenary indulgence *in articulo mortis*. Then we all recited the prayers for a happy death."

It seemed indeed that death could be only a matter of hours or even minutes away, but towards morning her breathing became easier and more regular. When she woke a few hours later she had recovered the power of speech, and turned to the nurse: "What are you doing here, *matota?*" – using a Piedmontese dialect word for "young woman".

She was not to die yet. Her separation from this life and from her Congregation would take time and would embrace a final learning process. Thecla was given eight months to review everything she had been taught during her life about humility, obedience, patience and courage. She had been Prima Maestra for 41 years – since that day in 1922 when Fr Alberione announced his choice among the pots and pans of the kitchen at Alba. She had become the self-taught Superior of a new-born community, learning something every day, until she herself was called on to counsel other superiors, to encourage priests: to teach others the ways of the spiritual life.

Each day had been an opportunity for learning; each day had had its conquests. And this for 41 years. But from the third Sunday in July 1963 the flow was reversed: every day saw something lost. She could move only with great difficulty; speech was often impossible; she could no longer write. Her life was becoming one long withdrawal. Many would have given themselves up to despair, but this was not Thecla's way. She quickly saw what her new situation was to be; she had accepted it from the beginning, and her consent was confirmed in the final words that her hand was able to trace on the page: "Lord, I want to do your will always and in all things."

This is not the account of the decline and dissolution of Prima Maestra Thecla Merlo but rather an account of the last lessons she had to learn. Fr Dragone, the priest who accompanied her in her final journey said that "throughout the eight months of her illness she was an example of Christian faith, hope and charity towards God and her neighbour".

She now had gradually to let go of all her old duties, to delegate, to let others take over. Perhaps during these moments she came to realise the extent of her achievements, the full weight of the burdens she had carried. For example, she had written no fewer than 8,000 letters. Like the heads of all religious institutes she was continually sending reports, requests and replies to the various offices of the Church. She engaged in correspondence with the bishops of every continent, at first to ensure a welcome for the Daughters (or at least to prevent their being sent back home); later to explain that she could send no more because the demand for their services was too great.

She must often have reflected on these continual requests from the bishops for more Daughters of St Paul, for it was in fact the fulfilment of a prophecy: "The Primo Maestro said that it would be like this."

Sometimes a bishop would come to make his case in person. The story is told of a prelate from the Ivory Coast who in 1960 arrived in the parlour to ask for sisters to open a Catholic book centre. Thecla was quite unable to spare anyone, but he insisted: "But this is Africa! Think of Africa!" And he went down on his knees. He was obviously a sick man, and yet he had come in person to ask for the Daughters' help. "The situation is pitiful", was all Thecla could say.

There were many other things to occupy the mind of a superior with houses in 24 different countries: correspondence, negotiations, meetings with individual bishops, with pontifical nuncios and with civil authorities. In addition there were the financial problems associated with every new enterprise; she was involved in decisions about purchasing, planning and construction projects all over the world. Such a work-load over so many years would have brought honour and fortune to any international manager, but for the Prima Maestra of the Daughters of St Paul this was just one part of the job – and not the most important. For her, the contact with individual sisters and superiors – a continuing dialogue in conferences, letters, circulars and personal meetings – counted for much more. All of these served the purpose of guiding her charges along the path to greatness, of "making them holy", as she never tired of saying.

She was greatly assisted in all these activities by the quality of her adjutants. But her talent for "management selection" sprang not from any organisational philosophy, but from the first virtue mentioned in the *Magnificat*, that humility which led her to seek help and even correction from others: "Please tell me what I should do..." "Thank you for helping me to understand", "Please excuse my rough manners; I'm not used to certain refinements..." That was how she excused herself to Angela Raballo (later Maestra Teresa in religion), whom she first met at Alba in 1916-17 at Canon Chiesa's catechism lessons. Angela was the young woman who led Fr Alberione's group of girls at Alba whilst the others were at Susa under Angela Boffi and Teresa Merlo. She later became head of the Pious Disciples and Superior of various communities.

In January 1963 they had found themselves together again at Alba, and Thecla asked her to tell the younger Daughters about the beginnings of the Pauline adventure. "After supper you must tell them all about the early days and everything you remember about the Founder." And then she herself sat there and listened "just like a child".

A week after her attack she began slowly to take food again, to put her feet on the ground and to spend a little time each day in a chair. Apart from the night of 16 June she remained completely lucid, and as her condition improved she was able to divide her day between treatment, pious practices and periods of rest. It was a real victory when she finally managed to move about a little, so that she could go into chapel for prayer before the Blessed Sacrament, and out onto the terrace for meditation.

A few days later she was strong enough to make journeys of a few hours to the General house in Rome and elsewhere to meet sisters and novices.

Pope Paul VI arrives at the clinic

On 22 August the Pope came over unexpectedly from Castelgandolfo to the clinic; it was one of the first visits of his pontificate and certainly the first to a Pauline house. His Holiness wanted both to comfort the suffering of the sick and to pay tribute to those who looked after them, spending time with the 200 or more patients, including sisters from every order and congregation. He celebrated Mass in the chapel, when he gave one of his most penetrating sermons. He began by greeting those who had founded the home: "Fr Alberione is here with us, as is the Superior of the Daughters of St Paul..." For Thecla was indeed present, and not as a patient: there is a photograph of the occasion which shows her standing next to the Pope wearing her habit. The Holy Father spoke about the situation of religious who had offered their whole lives to God only to see their sacrifice seemingly brought to nothing by illness, having to listen to words of comfort which merely confirmed that they were no longer capable of doing anything. "Just be quiet and rest... You don't have to worry about a thing..." His Holiness continued with these words: "Even in a home like this you can see the fearful pain and suffering this causes on the human level... the gulf that separates hope from reality. It is a wounding humiliation, a pain which denies those outgoing instincts with which we all affirm and express ourselves."

Maestra Thecla listened to these words of this Pope, so much younger than herself, and doubtless recognised her own situation and the thoughts expressed in her spiritual notes. His Holiness continued: "You have had a formation which enables you to understand that this type of consecration, this kind of offering of a life that has apparently been made useless, is in fact a very precious thing. There is a phrase of St Augustine's that has helped me on many occasions. I think it is one of the most illuminating that this great genius has left us, and he uses it with a profound sense of pity for those who do not understand the wisdom of the Gospel and the redemptive value of pain: *Amisistis utilitatem calamitatis: miserrimi facti estis* – You have lost the sense of the usefulness of pain and you have become the more wretched for it. If we were in fact to lose our sense of the value of toil, pain, tears, anguish and human death, what should we have become? The human spirit would have suffered a most dreadful defeat, and the pessimists would indeed have been proved right..."

These words would have awakened familiar echoes for Maestra Thecla, both recent and from the remoter past. There was something of Fr Alberione in the Holy Father's homily, something of Fr Pistone of Castagnito, of Canon Chiesa – even the voices of her first catechists, her parents Ettore and Vincenza Merlo. There is the doctrine of the Four Last Things, the eternal goal to which we are predisposed by the will of God; and now the Pope was summarising it all in these words: "It is in the light of the Gospel that suffering acquires meaning. There is a thought behind my existence and a design; there is co-ordination and a purpose. Nothing is a waste of time or effort, a pointless shedding of tears, a useless sacrifice, if it is given a value and a purpose."

It seemed almost as though the Pope was addressing her personally when he spoke of the value of suffering offered up for love: "This period of physical inactivity can even become more precious than the days of your prime to which you gave so much energy."

Some hours later Thecla was making this note in her spiritual notebook: "22/8 Immaculate Heart of Mary. Holy Father said Mass in the chapel at Albano Laziale. Ask Our Blessed Lady for her gift of humility, her love for Jesus and for the Church."

The chronicle of her illness and death records that she followed with great interest the progress of building work on the new wards and the church: "One evening at sunset we went onto the terrace of the ward currently under construction. 'Let's go and sprinkle a little holy water,' she said, and she moved off with Maestra Costantina and two other sisters. And whilst Maestra Costantina sprinkled the water she intoned the *Asperges*, and she continued to sing until the little ceremony was concluded. That frail voice from the silent terrace must surely have reached heaven; certainly the memory of it remains engraved on our hearts." This comes from the diary of her last months.

She felt she must try to serve the Pauline family even in this small way, by raising her voice at sunset over the Alban hills. Even the smallest gesture was precious to the apostolate; she had said so herself to generations of Daughters. But during this final period, when her mind went back so readily to the early days, perhaps she remembered having once listened to a similar message – about the value of any offering, however small, provided it was made with the right intention. Fr Alberione and Canon Chiesa had certainly made the point many times. But perhaps she recalled even more vividly the offering of the sweet-natured Clelia Calliano, the healthy young woman from Corneliano d'Alba, who succumbed to the Spanish flu in 1918 whilst Teresa Merlo and the others gathered around her bed to recite the fifth glorious mystery of the rosary. Clelia's last words were a promise: that if she lived she would devote herself with all her strength to the apostolate of the printed word – as cook, as housekeeper, in the humblest of roles. And in suffering too, as Maestra Thecla might now add.

Epilogue

THE UNFINISHED LAST ACT

"I'm only sorry I can't say good-bye to each one of you"

"I have learned that you can pass into the other world without noticing. You really aren't aware of it. I have been half-way, neither on this side nor the other; or at least so they told me, because I didn't realise where I was. And I said to them: 'See how quickly it can happen... We must always be ready for the journey, because you never know... like when you fall into a deep sleep and then you wake up... I'm only sorry I can't say good-bye to each one of you... They gave me permission to come...'"

Thecla was speaking in July 1963 during her first visit to the Roman community after her stroke: just a few words uttered in a feeble voice, ending with an invitation to recite the *Magnificat* together.

She spoke to them again on 23 September, her last visit to Rome. "They told me I could say a few words to you, so let it just be a few. We are all moving along the road to heaven, and those who are already there are waiting for us and praying for us. They have made their crossing from this world to the next; we are still on the way..." She devoted the whole of her short talk to the idea of the soul's journey towards the next life, one which other Daughters had already completed. "As the years pass there will always be those who go up there to increase the family."

Her thoughts were now entirely focused on that journey. Canon Chiesa was already "up there", having died in June 1946 after a life devoted to teaching and study. There were certain points from his instructions given in the church of SS Cosmas and Damian that Maestra Thecla could still remember by heart. The Canon, feeling he was about to die, had called for Fr Alberione, and his former pupil immediately rushed from Rome to be at his bedside. Each heard the other's confession, and the old man died a few days later. His last words of advice to the Primo Maestro were that he should have a special regard for Fr Giaccardo. But it was not long afterwards – on 24 January 1948 – that Giuseppe Timoteo Giaccardo himself went "up there". And so in the space of eighteen months the diminutive, fragile and yet indestructible Founder was deprived of the support of both his great counsellor and his most obedient lieutenant. He worked for the initiation in 1964 of the procedure for their beatification. On 11 December 1987 Canon Chiesa was declared "Venerable"; on 22 October 1989 Fr Giaccardo was declared "Blessed" ("Venerable" on 9 May 1985).

On 26 September Maestra Thecla went to Grottaferrata for a meeting of the superiors of the Congregation. It was the last time her words were recorded. She spoke for only a few minutes, and this time she chose not to talk about the next world; it was rather the address of a Prima Maestra to her high command, interspersed with personal observations on the theme of obedience.

Apart from the frailty of her voice, she seemed to be her old self for a few brief moments. Her words of encouragement recalled Maestra Thecla at the height of her powers: "When we obey and do what we are told, then indeed we have Our Lord's blessing, though things may look different to us – perhaps even the very opposite. For us this is an article of faith. Have they told us to do something? Then let us do it! And without 'ifs' or 'buts'. And if in the end things don't turn out as intended, Our Lord won't blame us for obeying but rather the person who gave the order. So always insist with the Daughters that we do as we are told."

Then she returned to the present. "I'm very glad to have been able to see you, and I hope this won't be the last time the good Lord allows me to greet you, because... I need a lot of patience. My head is no longer what it used to be." There was silence among the group of superiors as the last words trailed away. The Prima Maestra almost certainly realised that this was her real farewell; but even now she remained true to her usual style, unwilling, or unable, to give particular importance to the personal aspect of the occasion. And so they heard her say once again: "Be at peace! Are you all in good health? One or two of you look a little pale…"

She suffered the first stroke in June and for a time there were signs of a good recovery, but as the improvement slowed to a halt, Maestra Thecla became more withdrawn. She forgot people's names and had difficulty finding the right words. "I won't be going out any more," she murmured. "I can't remember enough to put a sentence together." She was in the prison of suffering, just as the Pope had described when he spoke in the chapel. Here was the pain that wounds and humiliates.

Taking part in the Paschal mystery

The Prima Maestra's problems had become more evident on 3 October, when she met a group of newly-professed sisters. Fr Dragone recalls: "Whilst we were speaking about our participation in the Paschal mystery – in the passion, death and resurrection, and in its grace and glory – her eyes, which never lost their brightness, became quite luminous… Speech came with great difficulty. She would begin a sentence and then almost immediately break off, looking in vain for the words to express her thought. She lost her way easily in conversation. It all caused her immense distress. She still had so many things to say and to do: projects to finish, others not yet begun."

Her spiritual notebook for 4 October reads: "Great trust in God, trust and confidence. He is a father who holds us in being, helps me, gives me everything. He is waiting for me in heaven. Do everything to please the heavenly Father. Mary help me! You were found pleasing to God…"

She got out of bed later now. She told Maestra Raballo:

"You know, I realised when I had the first stroke that I would have to wait six months to see if I was going to get over it, but it's still only five months. They didn't tell me that..."

Professor Ojetti observed that her eyes still burned with the light of a lively mind, and she continued to show a keen interest in the affairs of the Congregation. "Her expression was resigned and yet determined; it was the face of someone who looked with confidence towards the trial that lay ahead... But when she heard that any of her Daughters was unwell she became anxious and maternal. If I saw her after coming from the operating theatre she wanted news about every one of the patients. It was rather like 1945, when we carried out the first operations in the infirmary of the Generalate."

The Congregation now had Daughters drawn from several generations, with many different styles of living and working. Thecla, though she was fond of drawing lessons from certain historic moments in the life of the Congregation, never cast herself in the role of protagonist when speaking to her young postulants. At the same time she was anxious to promote those pioneer qualities that typified the small band who had been with her at Alba in the very beginning, so many of whom had already gone "up there" before her.

A small band indeed, but such a great one! They had met and overcome so many challenges. It seems incredible that at Fr Alberione's bidding they should have endured so much in exchange for so little. Young women in those days were expected to take the veil by joining time-honoured institutes with clearly-defined missions, established houses, a recognised habit and the honour and respect that goes with a long record of good works. The first Daughters appeared to be opting for a highly ambiguous condition. At first sight they were neither lay nor religious, and of the two ways of life they were taking on only the burdens. They had to work like ordinary lay women, but they also had to submit to religious discipline like members of a strict congregation. By throwing in their lot with Fr Alberione they began as seamstresses of military uniforms, graduating later to porters, brick-makers and paper-makers; and all this with no formal name or habit and living a clandestine life in rented lodgings.

This was their reward for taking at his word the diminutive James Alberione: "You will be new apostles, like none the world has ever seen before, but nevertheless essential to these times. You will be the indispensable Daughters of St Paul, and people from all over the world will beg for your help." He was saying this when not even the honest folk of Alba were prepared to acknowledge his mission as genuine, pitying these young women as victims of a madman.

The creation of a world wide Congregation from these unpromising beginnings was a miracle performed by a few for the benefit of a multitude. Those who now joined the Congregation found everything ready for them: they had an illustrious name; they wore their habit proudly; they had establishments in dozens of countries and a wide range of activities; they enjoyed fame and the satisfaction of feeling they were in the mainstream of history. But the Prima Maestra also knew what else awaited the new recruits: the hundreds of millions – half the human race – who were unaware of Christ; the gulf between what was so urgently needed and what was humanly possible, between their apostolic task and the forces they could muster. The vocation of the modern Daughter was every bit as challenging as in those early days at Alba, when their predecessors washed their clothes in the freezing stream, when the buildings lacked windows, when they kept themselves warm by wrapping up in shawls to go to church.

This was why the Prima Maestra, though she was drained of energy and unable to speak, did not want to miss these last chances of meeting her Daughters – the opening of the new refectory, the laying of the foundation stone of the new church, the traditional anniversary celebrations. She felt she must be there to offer her encouragement to the latest recruits as she had done over the years for so many others; for those who followed the Primo Maestro had much need of encouragement.

She knew that she could motivate the young merely by being there and – sick and weak as she was – by looking on in silence. In this she was following the example of another Daughter, Amabile Lombardi, who continued her apostolate after she became blind. Fr Battista Mabritto recalled her in these words: "She wanted to carry on working by having someone accompany her to places that she knew, where she could recognise people by their voices and books by their feel. She eventually died at the age of 42, and with the offering of her life she ensured the recovery of a sick postulant."

Sister Amabile, one of the great women who received their formation in humility at Thecla's hands, often repeated these words: "By myself I can do nothing, for I am nothing," which might seem merely an acknowledgement of weakness. But the words which complete the thought reveal the whole as a dynamic and liberating prayer: "But in God I can do all things."

On 14 October 1963 Thecla wrote in her spiritual notebook: "Lord, I thank you for making me realise that I am the most imperfect, wretched and stupid person and the greatest sinner in the world. Then I came to understand with the help of your grace that everything is arranged and permitted by you, whether it be my sickness, my weakness or my wretchedness; whatever happens is with your consent. My Jesus, I trust in you. Most holy Mary help me!"

This was not just an act of resignation by a sick woman: she had thought and spoken in this way throughout her life. When she accepted the duties of the apostolate she recognised that the only way to fulfil them was to stay close to God, or as she herself put it, "to leave the heart open to the work of grace". Whoever bases their apostolic efforts on an acceptance of their own worthlessness, whoever says with

St Paul, "I can do all things in him who strengthens me" (Phil 4:13), will always achieve results – today no less than in the past.

So she continued to teach others by her example of obedience, submitting with a smile to the more disagree-able procedures for the treatment for her condition. And what she taught was good-natured adjustment to the situation, not mere passive resignation.

It was the lesson of her whole life. In her writings she refers many times to hell and heaven, but there can be no doubt which of the two figures most prominently. She had no taste for the threat of eternal punishment. She used to say: "We mustn't live this vocation of ours in terror and anguish, but in love and with confidence in our heavenly Father." These words have been quoted before, but they find a special relevance to her months in the clinic as she lived under the threat of a possible relapse – in a few months, within days or at any moment.

"We must not live this vocation of ours in terror and anguish, but in love and with confidence in our Heavenly Father."

She never did anything to frighten the Daughters. To say that she loved them all deeply means very little; everyone has to be loved, within the convent or in the world outside. But for her Daughters she had a special feeling, a particular respect which she showed in all kinds of ways. She made a note of these principles in her diary: "Always think well of the sister and have great respect for her – even more than if you were standing next to the crucified Lord. She is the living image of God. We have a strong temptation to correct in others the faults we are most aware of in ourselves. I must deeply desire what is good for all of them, so that they become holy, happy and healthy… We must speak well of them all and not pay undue attention to their faults, but overlook them as we should want others to overlook our own."

Her three brothers came from Castagnito to visit her in

August, and Fr Costanzo celebrated Mass. She was enjoying her best health since the stroke and they found her calm and at peace, but she began to deteriorate soon afterwards and eventually suffered a relapse on 22 November.

The diary records that towards a quarter to eleven that morning "two nurses came to take an electro-cardiogram, entering the room one at a time on tiptoe to see if she was resting. But she was not. She was sitting on the bed looking extremely pale, and her eyes were wandering as though she were looking for something. She mumbled a few words, but we were unable to understand her." The nurses did what they could until the doctors arrived. She had clearly had another stroke, a milder attack but a longer one, and the effects were soon evident – a slight paralysis of the right-hand side.

Fr Alberione hurried to her side to administer the Sacrament of the Sick. She was quite conscious and had regained her composure. She looked around at everyone, but she could speak only with enormous difficulty. She just kept repeating: "Never mind... Let God's will be done... Thanks be to God! ...Oh dear me!"

God's will always and in everything

The final entry in her spiritual notebook is for 22 November, the day of her second stroke: "Lord, I want to do your will always and in all things: obedience to you in everything. My Guardian Angel, help me!"

Sister Nazarena Morando recalled: "She made various attempts to write, but each time she put down the pen and shook her head with tears in her eyes, gesturing as though to say she could do no more and bowed to God's will."

She was now almost unable to speak – another bitter blow to her prayer life. Sister Nazarena read passages to her from the Prayers of the Pauline Family: "When I had finished she used to look at me with a smile as though to thank me, and then she gathered herself in concentration. Once or twice, when she felt better, the nurses allowed her to make a brief visit to the chapel; I sometimes accompanied her myself. After a while I would go back to see if she was tired, and she would hold out her beads to show me that she hadn't finished her rosary, begging me with her eyes to let her stay a little longer. At the end she always came away cheerful and serene."

Sister Nazarena had more than one reason for staying close to Maestra Thecla. She was her Superior General, but in years gone by she had also been a mother to her. In the house in Rome Nazarena suffered from bronchial asthma and at night she was wracked with constant coughing, particularly in winter. It disturbed the other sisters, and this upset her very much. "The Prima Maestra told me to come and sleep in her room, and refused to listen to my objections: 'It doesn't bother me at all. Cough away to your heart's content and by all means burn some of that powder if you need to!' She was referring to something the doctor had prescribed for me, a preparation that you heated to give off a vapour which calmed my cough a bit. Every night I filled the room with this smoke and yet I still coughed for hours. The Prima Maestra never complained: 'You poor thing! Go ahead; do whatever you need to breathe better.' She put up with this inconvenience for years without ever showing any sign of tiredness. For me that comes close to heroism."

Maestra Nazarena dashed to Rome from Bolivia as soon as she heard the news of the relapse. They wept together a while, and then Maestra Thecla listened to her stories of the South American mission. Maestra Ignazia, Thecla's deputy, and Maestra Nazarena helped her each day with her prayers. Then one day in December there arrived a publication which caused enormous joy to everyone in that room. It was the text of the decree on the means of social communication which had just been approved by the second Vatican Council, named after the first words of its Latin text, *Inter mirifica*.

This was a great moment for the whole Pauline family,

and Maestra Thecla's smile showed that she was able to savour it to the full. Here then in the year 1963 the Catholic Church, united in Council, "believes its task involves employing the means of social communication to announce the good news of salvation and to teach men how to use them properly." It went on to lay down that pastors should instruct the faithful "so that by using these means they arrive at salvation and perfection, not only for themselves but also for the whole human family."

Many ironic glances must have been exchanged across the Prima Maestra's room on hearing those words. When Fr Alberione was making his first plans to provide Catholics with "these means" he could only talk about them in a whisper to Canon Chiesa in case anything should reach ecclesiastical ears.

But further on there was something even more interesting. Number 15 of *Inter mirifica* states: "Priests, religious and laity should be trained at once to meet the needs described above. They should acquire the competence needed to use these media for the apostolate."

At once, indeed! It had taken the insistence of a Pope – Pius XI with his strong desire for a congregation dedicated to the press – to overcome the prejudices and suspicions of those who considered Alberione a megalomaniac who needed to be stopped as soon as possible. Now they were asking for it to be done at once!

Perhaps Maestra Thecla thought about the thousands of miles covered by the Daughters of St Paul across every continent, in peace, in war and in the middle of revolutions. Perhaps she remembered the lack of understanding of so many of the bishops they encountered, the accusation of being useless (if not actually dangerous) as the sisters pioneered the mission which, thirty years later, was judged to be so necessary, so urgent, something to be set in motion at once – as though a decree were enough to produce apostles.

James Alberione was also among the Council Fathers as

one of the Superiors General. He would undoubtedly have had things to tell his colleagues – what he had had to listen to and endure because he had understood fifty years earlier that certain matters ought to be tackled at once. But the function of the prophet is to speak out; not to tell people later "I told you so!"

From time to time, with the help of one of the sisters, Thecla managed to walk very slowly to the chapel of the clinic and say a few prayers, always concluding with her favourite ejaculation: "Thanks be to God!"

The diary continues: "Towards the end of January she was moved to a small apartment in the new extension named after the Guardian Angels. She looked almost sprightly as she got out of her wheel-chair and explored her new quarters. She usually managed to spend a few hours in her little study, sitting in an armchair or at her writing table. What joy it gave us as we saw her like that! It seemed almost as though she was back at work…"

In fact she was slowly losing her remaining strength. On 5 February she was no longer able to get out of bed and the doctors said that it would be inadvisable for Maestra Ignazia to leave the hospital. So it was that as she was coming out of the sick-room after one of her visits, she heard Thecla call her back. She returned to the bed side and the sick woman reached out to bless and embrace her. And so, with this typically simple gesture, Maestra Thecla handed over to her faithful deputy the Congregation of the Daughters of St Paul.

A little later she made a sign that she was feeling unwell again and the doctors were called to relieve her pain. "Do you feel better?" they asked, and with staring eyes she answered "No… no…"

Her brothers, Fr Alberione and Fr Dragone were called for, and the medical staff stood by. About midday she suffered another stroke, quickly followed by two more. Further attacks followed later and it was clear that she was nearing the end. Fr Alberione asked one of the Daughters to read the Gospel account of the Passion. There was no sound in the room apart from the subdued tones of the reader, punctuated by the ring of familiar names: the *praetorium*, Gethsemane, Calvary...

Teresa Merlo, Thecla in religion, Prima Maestra of the Daughters of St Paul, died at four o'clock in the afternoon of Wednesday, 5 February 1964, just two weeks before her seventieth birthday.

Across the world

"You will have another Superior General but not another mother," was Fr Alberione's comment to the Daughters.

The funeral was marked by a most beautiful gesture: the heavy coffin was carried to the hearse by a party of Daughters of St Paul before it left for the Verano cemetery in Rome.

Exactly three years later, on 5 February 1967, her body was brought "home" to be buried in the sub-crypt of the *Regina Apostolorum* sanctuary. On this return journey the coffin was carried for part of the way by eight men of the Society drawn from different countries. Maestra Thecla had been a mother to them too.

The Daughters have continued to follow in her wake across the world. They are now present in 38 countries and on every continent, and they bring into God's service those means of communication which, in the wrong hands, can sow the seeds of ruin. This was why for so long the Church feared them, neglected them and ignored them. What was required was a Thecla, someone with too much trust in God to be afraid of anything on this earth; it called for a truly thoughtful person to guide so many women to an understanding of the new technologies and to enrich them with the spirit. What was needed was her gentle style of leadership.

This was the phrase James Alberione used to describe her style; and it is with his words that we conclude this account of a woman endowed to a heroic degree with a rich array of virtues – Maestra Thecla, Servant of God.

"The Prima Maestra saw everything in God; saw everything as coming from God, everything ordained by God, all her actions were directed towards the glory of God. When a soul reaches this point it is ready to enter heaven, because heaven is the glorification of God.

"Hers was a contemplative soul; she prayed continuously and found union with the Lord anywhere and everywhere. Her spirit was finely tempered. She was illuminated by a light that glowed ever brighter... She listened, pondered and mulled things over, particularly towards the end of her life. The sole purpose of her existence was to promote God's glory. This is the pinnacle of holiness... As I have said on other occasions, holiness in its very highest form consists in seeking the glory of God in everything. The Prima Maestra undoubtedly achieved that supreme degree of dedication."

Chronological notes

1894 *20 February:* MARIA TERESA MERLO is born at Castagnito, Province of Cuneo, the second of the four children of Ettore and Vincenza Merlo (née Rolando).

 22 February: She is baptised in the parish church of St John the Baptist by Fr Pietro Palladino.

1901-1903 She attends the village school at Castagnito, which offers only the first three years of elementary education. Her parents send her to study with a private teacher, Maria Chiarla.

1902 *23 April:* She makes her first Holy Communion in the parish church of Castagnito.

1903 *29 July:* Death of Pope Leo XIII.

 9 August: Election of Giuseppe Sarto as Pope Pius X.

1907 *29 September:* She receives the sacrament of Confirmation in the parish church of Castagnito at the hands of Bishop Giuseppe Francisco Re of Alba.

1918-1911 She learns tailoring and embroidery with the Sisters of St Ann at the Retreat House of the Divine Providence at Alba. Her parents later send her to Turin to improve her skills.

1912 She sets up a small workshop to teach sewing and embroidery to young girls in the family home.

1914 *28 June:* Assassination at Sarajevo of Archduke Ferdinand, heir to the throne of Austria-Hungary, with his wife Sophia. This is the spark that leads to the outbreak just over a month later of the first world war.

 20 August: Death of Pius X. On the same day Fr Alberione opens the Young Workers' Printing School, the seedling that was eventually to grow into the Society of St Paul.

 6 September: Giacomo della Chiesa is elected Pope and takes the name of Benedict XV.

1915 *24 May:* Italy enters the war against Austria-Hungary.

 15 June: Fr James Alberione opens the women's workshop in Piazza Cherasca, Alba, in the premises vacated by the young men of the Printing School. This date marks the birth of the Daughters of St Paul.

	27 June: Teresa meets Fr Alberione in the sacristy of the parish church of SS Cosmas and Damian at Alba.
1915-1918	Teresa and her companions join the League of Catechists of the parish of SS Cosmas and Damian and attends courses of religious doctrine under the direction of Canon Chiesa. She teaches catechism.
1916	*29 June:* Fr Alberione receives her temporary private vows.
1918	*15 October:* Fr Alberione meets Bishop Giuseppe Castelli of Susa to discuss the revival of the diocesan newspaper, *La Valsusa.*
	4 November: End of the Italian conflict with Austria-Hungary.
	11 November: End of fighting on all fronts of the first world war.
	18 December: The small community of two young women and three girls moves from Alba to Susa to produce the diocesan newspaper.
1922	*22 January:* Death of Pope Benedict XV.
	6 February: Achille Ratti is elected Pope as Pius XI.
	22 July: Teresa, together with eight other young women, takes perpetual private vows and adopts the religious name of Maestra Thecla. These professions mark the institution of the Pious Society of the Daughters of St Paul. Fr Alberione appoints her Superior General.
	28 October: The Fascist march on Rome. Benito Mussolini, leader of the Fascist movement, becomes head of the Italian government.
1923	*23 March:* The small community finally leaves Susa and returns to Alba.
1924	*10 February:* Fr Alberione founds the Pious Disciples of the Divine Master.
1926	*January:* Foundation of the Pauline house in Rome.
1928	*30 October:* With a group of other sisters Maestra Thecla dons the habit of the Daughters of St Paul for the first time.
	November: The first branch houses are opened at Salerno, Bari and Verona. Maestra Thecla personally accompanies the sisters and helps them during the early stages. This work marks the beginning of her missionary journeys.

1929	**11 February:** Concordat between the Kingdom of Italy and the Catholic Church.
	15 March: Bishop Re recognises the Daughters of St Paul as a congregation of diocesan right. In the decree Maestra Thecla is named Superior General with the title of Prima Maestra.
	October: The beginning of the economic crisis in the USA, which later extends to Europe with grave consequences.
1933	**January:** In Germany, Adolf Hitler, leader of the Nazi party, is appointed Chancellor; within a year he becomes President of the Republic.
	November: At Borgo Piave, Alba, the Daughters of St Paul move from the quarters they have so far occupied next to those of the Pauline priests and brothers and take up residence in a new building, which becomes their Mother house.
1936	**26 March–27 August:** Thecla sails from Genoa on the *Augustus* for her first overseas journey, when she visits the communities in Brazil, Argentina and the USA.
	11 November: Maestra Thecla moves to Rome.
1937	**28 January –6 March:** She visits the New York house, travelling there and back on the liner *Rex.*
	July: Start of the eight-year Sino-Japanese war.
1939	**10 February:** Death of Pope Pius XI.
	2 March: Election of Eugenio Pacelli as Pope Pius XII.
	1 September: The German attack on Poland marks the beginning of the second World War.
1940	**10 June:** Italy enters the war.
1941	**9 March:** Death of Thecla's father, Ettore Merlo.
1943	**25 July–8 September:** The fall of Mussolini culminates in an armistice between Italy and the Allies.
	21 October: She welcomes into the Generalate at Rome the 26 Benedictine nuns who have been forced by the war to leave their monastery at Monte Cassino. They remain until 18 August 1944.
	13 December: The Holy See issues the *Decretum Laudis*, granting provisional Vatican recognition to the Daughters of St Paul.

1945	*September:* End of the second World War.

28 December - 23 May 1946: Maestra Thecla embarks at Naples with the Founder on the *Andrea Gritti*, bound for the United States. She continues to Argentina and Brazil.

1946	*2–3 June:* Birth of the Italian Republic, following a referendum.

1947	*18 January:* Death of Thecla's mother, Vincenza Merlo (née Rolando).

3 April: Bishop Luigi Grassi recognises the Pious Disciples of the Divine Master as a congregation of diocesan right.

1949	*3 April–24 July:* Thecla accompanies the Founder on a round-the-world journey through India, the Philippines, Japan, Mexico and the United States.

30 September–11 October: She visits the communities in France and Spain.

1 October: Proclamation in Peking of the Chinese People's Republic, following which the communist regime soon begins to banish all foreign missionaries and attempts to subject the Chinese Church to the State.

1952	*21 March–14 June:* Maestra Thecla makes another tour of the American houses with the Founder, visiting the United States, Canada, Mexico, Chile, Argentina and Brazil. She encourages the idea of short catechetical films and provides vital financial help for their production.

12–26 July: She visits the houses in France.

Regular black-and-white television transmissions begin in Italy – on one channel only until 1961.

1953	*15 March:* The Holy See confers full pontifical recognition on the Congregation of the Daughters of St Paul and approves its Constitutions.

13 April–22 May: Maestra Thecla accompanies the Founder on another tour of the houses of the Far East: Japan, Philippines and India.

13 July–3 September: She again travels with Fr Alberione to the Americas, visiting the houses in Canada, United States, Colombia, Chile, Argentina and Brazil.

5–10 September: The second National Council of Mothers General is held in Rome. Maestra Thecla is elected to preside over FIRAS, the Italian federation of women religious working in the field of community care.

1–18 November: She visits the communities in France, Spain and Portugal.

1955   *16 April - 2 June:* Thecla makes another journey to the Far East with the Founder, covering the Philippines, Japan, Australia and India.

27 July–22 August: She visits the European houses: the United Kingdom, France, Spain and Portugal.

12 September–12 December: She travels again to the Americas with Fr Alberione: the United States, Canada, Mexico, Colombia, Chile, Argentina and Brazil.

1956   *25–31 July:* Maestra Thecla visits the Great Britain and Spain.

1957   *7 January:* She summons the first General Chapter of the Daughters of St Paul, which is held from 4 to 7 May.

23 February: She undergoes a radical mastectomy at the *Regina Apostolorum* Clinic at Albano Laziale.

4 May: She is re-confirmed as Superior General for a further period of 12 years by the first General Chapter.

1958   *9 October:* Pope Pius XII dies at Castelgandolfo.

28 October: Angelo Giuseppe Roncalli suceeds as Pope John XXIII.

1959   *14 September–13 February 1960:* Maestra Thecla, together with the Superior General of the Pious Disciples of the Divine Master, visits the houses of the United States, Canada, Mexico, Venezuela, Colombia, Chile, Argentina and Brazil.

1960   *5–11 August:* She visits the community in London.

18 September–1 October: She visits the community in Spain.

1961   *12 April:* The first human flight in space is announced by the Russians. Yuri Gagarin circles the earth in the spaceship *Vostok* I.

28 May: At Ariccia, south of Rome, during the spiritual exercises for the feast of the Holy Trinity, Maestra Thecla offers her life for the sanctification of the Daughters of St Paul.

November: She visits the houses in Kinshasa, Zaire.

1962

24 January–19 May: Maestra Thecla makes her last journey to the Far East, visiting India, the Philippines, Taiwan, Japan, Korea and Australia.

20 February: The American, John Glenn, makes three orbits of the earth on board the spaceship *Mercury-Friendship 7.*

5 August - 3 September: She visits the houses in the United States and Canada.

11 October: Pope John XXIII opens the second Ecumenical Council of the Vatican in St Peter's Rome.

1963

8–17 May: Maestra Thecla's last overseas journey takes her to Kinshasa and Lubumbashi in Zaire. She returns on 17 May.

3 June: Death of Pope John XXIII.

16 June: Thecla suffers a stroke.

21 June: Giovanni Battista Montini is elected Pope and takes the name of Paul VI.

22 August: Thecla is overjoyed at meeting Pope Paul VI, who visits her in the *Regina Apostolorum* Clinic.

22 November: Thecla suffers another stroke. Fr Alberione administers the Sacrament of the Sick.

John F Kennedy, President of the United States, is assassinated at Dallas, Texas, and is succeeded by the Vice-president, Lyndon B Johnson.

4 December: The second Ecumenical Council of the Vatican approves the decree on the means of social communication, *Inter mirifica.*

1964

5 February: Maestra Thecla dies at Albano Laziale in the *Regina Apostolorum* Clinic following a cerebral haemorrhage. Fr Alberione gives her spiritual comfort at the end.

1967

26 October: The opening stages of the process in view of the eventual beatification and canonisation of Maestra Thecla begins in the Vicariate in Rome. It concludes on 23 March 1968

1992

22 January: Pope John Paul II signs the decree which recognises the heroic character of Maestra Thecla's virtues, and confers on her the title of Venerable.

Further reading in English

A Woman for Our Time, by Spartaco Lucarini (St Paul Editions, Boston 1974)

Thoughts, James Alberione, A Marvel of This Century, (St Paul Publications, England 1984)

James Alberione: Apostle For Our Times, by Luigi Rolfo, SSP (Staten Island, NY: Alba House 1987)

Blessed Timothy Giaccardo, An Obedient Prophet, by Eugenio Fornasari, SSP (Staten Island, NY: Alba House 1991)

Evangelii Nuntiandi, on Evangelization in the Modern World, an Apostolic Exhortation of Paul VI, 1975

Mulieris Dignitatem, on the Dignity and Vocation of Women, an Apostolic Letter of John Paul II, 1988

Christifideles Laici, on the Vocation and Mission of Lay People, an Encyclical Letter of John Paul II, 1988

Redemptoris Missio, on the Missionary Mandate, an Encyclical Letter of John Paul II, 1990

Pastores Dabo Vobis, I Will Give You Shepherds, an Encyclical Letter of Pope John Paul II, 1992

Aetatis Novae, on Social Communications, a Pastoral Instruction by the Pontifical Council for Social Communications, 1992

Index